Majestic Journey

AN IDITAROD DOG TEAM GIVES A ROOKIE MUSHER A 1,000 MILE RIDE OF HIS LIFE ACROSS REMOTE ALASKA

BILL JACK

PUBLICATION
CONSULTANTS
We Believe In The Power Of Authors

PO Box 221974 Anchorage, Alaska 99522-1974
books@publicationconsultants.com, www.publicationconsultants.com

ISBN Number: 978-1-59433-974-5
eBook ISBN Number: 978-1-59433-975-2

Library of Congress Number: 2020920162

Front cover photo ©Jeff Schultz/SchultzPhoto.com

Manufactured in the United States of America

ACKNOWLEDGMENTS

I thank the many people who willingly helped me before the race, during the race and writing this book. Thank you Ray Lang for your help and some colorful advice for running the race. Thank you the late Rahn Parker and the late George Parkhurst and the late Doc Leedy for all your help. A special thank you to the late Mark LaChapelle and his wife Penny and their son Elliott for your help and endless hospitality, opening up your home to us for several days before the race. Thank you Jerry and Sherell Holtzhouser in McGrath, Junie and Linda Towarak in Unalakleet and Walter Sagoonik in Shaktoolik for your warm hospitality at your homes. Thank you Penny for your unending support and patience that made this dream come true. Thank you Thurman for the many hours you put in, nightly feeding the dogs and your help before and after training runs. Thank you Mori and Dana for doing your house chores so we had more time to prepare for the race. Thank you my three sons, Joe, Tom and Thurman, for your help during the summer dog team runs with the ATV. In addition, thank you to the hundreds of volunteers who make this race happen every year. I especially want to thank my daughter in law, Nancy Jack, for all the direction she offered me concerning this book.

CONTENTS

FOREWORD
BY JEFF SCHULTZ

Official Photographer of Alaska's Iditarod since 1982 I'm convinced there is absolutely no one in the world who can fathom the unequivocal demands that the body, mind and soul endures, as a musher crossing Alaska by dog team. The sleep deprivation, the constant gnaw of the cold, the unending chores of feeding & watering the animals, the fear of upcoming trail conditions, the need to be everything to their dog team (provider, navigator, inspirational coach) and what seems like an endless white confinement of trail. The Iditarod dog musher must endure & conquer through it all, in extreme conditions.

Though I've mushed dog teams over my years of involvement, I've never run the Iditarod. My understanding of the Iditarod comes after travelling the trail forty times via plane and snow machine and from intersecting with hundreds of mushers in countless trail locations and nearly every imaginable situation; mental, physical, geographic, weather and emotional.

Having first-hand experience of the Iditarod for so many years, I contend that EVERY person who travels the trail; volunteer or musher, could write a book of their memories on any given year. There are THAT many adventures mishaps, close calls, unique people, and tales that every musher will encounter, travelling the Iditarod trail. It's to these exact same things that Bill Jack has put down his personal memories in Majestic Journey. I can certainly understand why Bill chose those two words for his book; Majestic Journey.

Majestic: adjective: possessing majesty; of lofty dignity or imposing aspect; stately; grand - Sliding on the runners for hours and hours through the 6,000 ft. peaks of the Alaska Range and crossing Rainy Pass would certainly connote majesty. Experiencing the infinitely vast, untouched and diverse remaining miles of Alaska wilderness God created would as well.

Journey: noun; a traveling from one place to another, usually taking a rather long time; trip: passage or progress from one stage to another. - A typical mushing "journey" of the Iditarod will likely be 8-13 days for most mushers today, from Alaska's Southcentral area, to the interior and finally to the Bering Sea Coast. But much more so, the progress and stages it took him, as a human being, to be truly and constantly "in the moment" and present, each of his senses on high-alert, experiencing and being the main character in his adventure.

I think you'll understand his experience and passion more as you put yourself inside his head when you read about he and his sled careening around a blind corner and catapulting him off the sled, where he watched (no doubt in slow motion) his sled twisting 360 degrees in mid-air. And later in the race, to his complete surprise, he and his team were bucking a 40 mph headwind with blowing snow creating a milk-bottle affect. He had to put all his faith and trust in his lead dogs to find the trail.

It's the daily adventure of this kind of experience that most of us will never know if it weren't for a story like this. Next to driving a team of dogs to Nome yourself, Majestic Journey, will get you as close to the runners as you can get. Enjoy the journey—

KEY

- Checkpoint
- - - - - - Route traveled in even-numbered years
- - - - - - Route traveled in odd-numbered years
——— Route traveled in all years

IDITAROD CHECKPOINTS

1991 Southern Route - *

1. Anchorage
2. Eagle River
3. Wasilla
4. Knik
5. Skwentna
6. Finger Lake
7. Rainy Pass
8. Rohn
9. Nikolai
10. McGrath
11. Takotna
12. Ophir
13. Iditarod - *
14. Shageluk - *
15. Anvik - *
16. Grayling - *
17. Eagle Island - *
18. Kaltag
19. Unalakleet
20. Shaktoolik
21. Koyuk
22. Elim
23. White Mountain
24. Safety
25. Nome

1992 Northern Route - *

1. Anchorage
2. Eagle River
3. Wasilla
4. Knik
5. Skwentna
6. Finger Lake
7. Rainy Pass
8. Rohn
9. Nikolai
10. McGrath
11. Takotna
12. Ophir
13. Cripple - *
14. Ruby - *
15. Galena - *
16. Nulato - *
17. Kaltag
18. Unalakleet
19. Shaktoolik
20. Koyuk
21. Elim
22. White Mountain
23. Safety
24. Nome

INTRODUCTION

Traveling across the vast Alaskan wilderness on a dogsled was exhilarating. There were nights when I could turn off my headlight and let the moon light the trail ahead. On other clear nights, I was awed, watching the Northern Lights dancing across the sky. During the day, the beauty of this remote wilderness was absolutely awesome to behold.

In contrast, the challenges were many. A musher must cook, feed and take care of the dogs with no outside help. The lack of sleep, freezing temperatures and the demands of the trail are exhausting. Mushers are tested physically, mentally and emotionally. Many times the unexpected suddenly happens. It could be an angry moose, a broken sled, a serious injury, frostbite, a life threatening blizzard, losing your team or even being run over by a snow machine (snowmobile).

The Iditarod is the ultimate test of endurance, stamina and perseverance for the dog driver and his team of dogs. Majestic Journey will show you what it's like to ride the runners of a dogsled day and night for two solid weeks across our country's last frontier.

CHAPTER 1

BRIEF HISTORY

"The only impossible journey is the one you never begin."

Tony Robbins

The Iditarod Sled Dog Race is known as a 1,049-mile race from Anchorage to Nome, Alaska. The 1,000 refers to the approximate length of the race, and the 49 refers to Alaska being the 49th state. Every year, the race is scheduled to start the first Saturday in March. The race trail follows the old mail and freight routes used by dog team carriers from the late 1800s through the early 1900s. There were cabins and roadhouses about every 25 miles. During the winter, these hearty mushers were constantly moving across remote Alaska hauling the mail and freight in and out of Alaskan villages and mining camps.

The late Joe Redington Sr. and the late Dorothy Page are respectfully the Father and Mother of the Iditarod. They both lived in the Wasilla area, which is about 45 miles North of Anchorage. Dorothy was a historian and Joe was an early homesteader who had a kennel of sled dogs. For years, people had hired Joe and his dog team to haul supplies for them into areas where there were no roads. He knew what a unique and incredible animal these sled dogs were. When the snow machines were invented and sold throughout Alaska in the 1960s, the sled dog numbers drastically declined and were on the verge of becoming extinct. Joe became very concerned.

In the late 1960's, Joe thought a sled dog race across Alaska would bring the sled dogs back. Dorothy heard about what Joe was proposing and became very interested. She thought this would be a wonderful opportunity for people to become more aware of the colorful frontier history that existed in the early 1900s. She was sure the race would be an intriguing and tangible link to the past. They became friends and worked tirelessly promoting this dream.

People continually told them they were crazy. The roadhouses that provided rest stops for the early dog teams and their drivers were long gone. Many told Joe and Dorothy that logistically, it would be impossible to organize a race of such magnitude through the vast remoteness of the Alaskan wilderness.

For years, Joe and Dorothy were persistent looking for support. They were convinced of its importance and overcame many hurdles before it finally became a reality in 1973. The Iditarod has grown over the years in popularity. Congress declared it a national historic trail in 1976. Some years, there are as many as 80 teams that sign up to run.

Television and the media have helped to promote the race. Many businesses and companies help sponsor the Iditarod and individual mushers as well. The Iditarod Trail Organization is now a multi-million-dollar business that employs several full time employees at the Iditarod Headquarters in Wasilla, Alaska. In addition, thousands of volunteers make this unique event happen every year.

Joe Redington's vision of bringing back the sled dogs to the state has become a reality in an enormous way. There are now many more sled dog races ranging from 10 to 1,000 miles throughout Alaska. Thousands of sled dogs now exist and many people have recreational dog teams just for the love of dogs and the exhilaration of riding behind these amazing animals.

Joe died on June 12, 1999 at the age of 82 after entering the race for many years. Dorothy died on November 16, 1989, at the age of 68. Both enjoyed many years of watching the Iditarod come to fruition. They will long be remembered.

CHAPTER 2

RACE PREPARATION

"Iditarod racers keep a schedule of Olympic athletes to train their animals and then tack on the schedule of a farmer to take care of them."

Martin Buser – An Iditarod four time Champion

Living in Nome, Alaska, I became fascinated watching Iditarod mushers finish every year. I started collecting sled dogs in 1982. My first sled dog was a four-year old, Siberian husky from Saint Lawrence Island (Close to Siberia). The dog was a small 40-pound leader and his name was Duke Ellington. I found Duke and the Siberian husky, to have a very thick undercoat, which was great for staying warm. Unfortunately, the thick undercoat caused him to heat up and run slow during daytime runs. At night, however, he was incredibly fast. During many of my 200 to 300 mile races, he became my night-shift leader. Some of those races, I would give him a free ride in the sled during daylight hours.

In 1986, I was running the Kobuk 220 race out of Kotzebue, Alaska. After the first 30 miles, we mushed into the first checkpoint at Snyder's Camp, with Duke in the sled. When a musher had a dog in the sled, it usually meant that the dog was being dropped to be cared for at the checkpoint. The checker asked if I wanted to drop the dog I was carrying. I said, "no, he's my night shift." Never hearing the phrase, "he's my night shift," the checker started laughing and couldn't wait to tell some of the spectators about my strategy.

I decided I needed faster dogs and especially a speedy leader. I was able to purchase a fast lead dog-named Pepper. She had originally come from the late Susan Butcher's dog lot. Susan had placed either first or second in the Iditarod, seven different years. I bred Pepper with a tough, experienced race dog named Moose that I had purchased from the late Herbie Nayokpuk. Herbie had finished the Iditarod in the top eight finishers, seven different years. From that breed came Cheetah. Cheetah became a lead dog when she was only one and a half year old. One of her first races in lead, she won a two-day, 40 mile dog sled race. You will read more of her incredible accomplishes in this book.

Penny and I continued to raise and race sled dogs. We enjoyed running the dog teams across the wide-open barren land that surrounded Nome, Alaska and the Seward Peninsula. We had fun and success racing in the local sprint races each weekend that the Nome Kennel Club would put on during the first three months of each year. I also had participated in many 200 and 300-mile dog sled races over those eight years. Most all of our dogs were bred and raised in our dog lot and were between two and eight years old. The challenge of mushing the Iditarod had intrigued me for years. Working full-time as a physical education teacher and basketball coach at Nome Public Schools, family responsibilities and finances, never allowed me the chance.

Around the beginning of November of 1990, Penny said "1991 should be the year for you to run the Iditarod." I answered, "I don't think so." She insisted, "our dogs are in their prime and if you don't do it this year, it may never happen." She continued, "ten years from now, you will regret not doing it when you had the chance." Penny was working for Alaska Airlines, but said she would help me train on the weekends. We decided to do it.

The logistics of preparing for this would be monumental. We were so busy that our first 20-mile training run did not happen until Thanksgiving weekend. Our dogs were in pretty good shape from our twice a week fun runs during the Summer and Fall. During those seasons, we would harness and hook them up to an ATV four-wheeler. There were many trails that we could access out of our dog lot that was next to our home.

To run the Iditarod though, 1,000 miles of training was necessary. To be ready by the first of March, I had to make the most of literally every mile of training. I decided that we needed to put the following training miles in; 200 miles in December, 300 in January and 400 in February. We were blessed to have mountains close by. Some of those runs would be pulling a heavy load up and over mountains to help toughen the dogs' strength.

I also realized that I needed to get in excellent physical condition. I remember Joe Runyan, a former Iditarod champion, emphasizing the importance of being in tip-top condition to run the Iditarod. He once told me, "there are times you work 16-hour days and sometimes 48-hours straight, and this goes on for two weeks." He continued, "mushers that are in the best of condition suffer much less than those who are not."

I taught a few classes at the swimming pool at the Nome High School, so it was convenient for me to utilize the facility. The swimming would strengthen my knees, increase my cardiovascular capacity and get my upper body prepared for the constant maneuvering of the heavy sled, through 100 miles of the Alaska Range.

During the Iditarod, our school district had Spring break and I also had four days of personal leave built up. I still needed a few extra days of approved leave. I was relieved the first of December when I was granted permission to take the necessary days off. I found a substitute teacher to cover for me. One of the requirements to enter the race was to have finished a 200-mile race. I had completed many of those in the past, so that was another hurdle I had already crossed. I then sent in my required paperwork along with the $1,249 entry fee to the Iditarod headquarters.

I did a lot of my training at night after getting home from coaching basketball practice. To strengthen the dogs, I used a heavy snow machine sled with iron runners and dragged a large truck tire going out. At the halfway point, I would lift the tire into the sled and the team would continue a fast trot back to our dog lot. This tactic increased their strength and speed. It was usually 10 p.m. by the time the training and chores were over. On the weekends and all through Christmas vacation, Penny and I enjoyed going out together and running two teams of nine dogs each. The extra time off from school allowed us to easily reach our 200 miles of training for the month of December.

Once school started up in January, the mileage goals would be more difficult to accomplish. Every other weekday, I would hook all 18 dogs that I was considering taking on the Iditarod. At times, my tight schedule required going out into some pretty nasty weather. I think this was helping my team to feel confident about running in blizzard type conditions. I have heard mushers say more than once, "prepare for the worst and hope for the best."

January was a busy month. I made basketball trips to Bethel, Kotzebue and Dillingham with the high school boys' team. All our competition was 300 to 600 miles away that required chartering a nine passenger aircraft. If our Nome boys' team were flying to Bethel, the charter would bring the Bethel girls team back to Nome. This made travel costs affordable with both schools paying for half the air charter.

While we were competing in Kotzebue, my dad, who was 80 years old and lived in Florida, had a serious heart attack. My four siblings and I met in Florida, thinking he may not make it. While in the ICU, he slowly started improving. My Dad eventually recovered and lived eight more active years to the age of 88.

After five days there, I felt there was no way I could recover the miles of training that were missed. Penny called on the sixth day I was there and informed me that my good friend, the late Rahn Parker, had taken all eighteen of my dogs on a seventy mile training run. I was overjoyed, knowing we were back on schedule. After arriving home, I was able to get two quality runs in before flying to Dillingham for basketball. While in Dillingham, my team qualified for the state tournament to be held in Fairbanks the first part of February. I was happy for my team, but this added more stress to my already tight schedule.

During this heavy training, the dogs were given about two pounds of frozen fish in the morning. This was like a popsicle to them. At night after their run, they would receive a hot meal. I was giving the dogs the food I was going to feed them during the race so their digestive system would be well adjusted to the change in diet. My son, Thurman, who was 12 years old, did much of the feeding. It was his preferred family chore. He also helped to put on and take off harnesses before and after training runs. His assistance was invaluable.

Three weeks before the race, the dog food drops were due in Anchorage. The Iditarod Trail Committee sends an Iditarod musher, heavy-duty bags for the food drops. Each bag had the checkpoint name in large letters. I added my name so I could easily find it, when entering a checkpoint. I had ordered 2,000 pounds of frozen beef, lamb, white fish, salmon, chicken skins. Our good friend, the late George Parkhurst, had a ban saw and helped me slice up all the meat and fish, which would allow for a faster snack time during the race.

One weekend, I placed 52 bags (two for each checkpoint) in a row on our wrap around deck. My seven and ten year old daughters, Dana and Mori, enjoyed helping me fill each large bag with many smaller bags of each variety of meat, fish, commercial dog food, extra batteries for my headlamp and a bag of about 60 dog booties for each checkpoint. In addition, my meals were added. There were dinner meals that Penny had prepared for me in seal-a-meal bags. When boiling water for the dogs, all I had to do was drop the seal-a-meal dinner into the boiling water to heat it up. I also added a couple small bags of trail mix to each checkpoint bag for my snacking.

I didn't have the money to purchase a new sled, so I ordered a longer and wider Teflon bottom for my toboggan dogsled. This made for a much larger and sturdier sled to use in the race. I also had to make tug lines that connect from the towline to the dog's harness. The towline runs through the middle of the team and is connected to the sled. Airplane cable was required to run through the inside of the towline to make it chew proof. Ray Lang, a Nome friend and Iditarod finisher, lent me the tools I needed to complete the task.

Ray also made me a very efficient square box cooker out of aluminum. Inside and at the bottom of the cooker, I placed an insulated pie pan filled with house insulation to soak up the liquid fuel. After 12 ounces of Heet (liquid fuel) was added to the insulation and lit, a three-gallon pot filled with water was placed inside the cooker. When the hinged lid of the cooker was closed, the water came to a boil in about 15 minutes. The Iditarod Organization furnished mushers with small bottles of Heet at every checkpoint.

Time went by quickly and all of a sudden it was only two weeks before the start of the race. The team had been building strength, endurance and speed, but I needed another 200 more training miles. My Iditarod team was now down to 17 dogs. The 1991 Iditarod rules allowed a musher to start with as many as 20 dogs. Since then, the rules now (2020), require a musher to start with no more than 14 dogs. With smaller dog teams in the race today, this helps mushers, vets and Iditarod management to better care for the dogs.

I decided the final test would be a 150-mile run to White Mountain and back on the Iditarod Trail. I left our dog lot at 6 p.m. on a Friday night (February 15). The team ran well that night arriving into White Mountain at 2 a.m. I rested the team on the riverbank where the Iditarod teams check in and rest every year. After about an hour, I cooked a hot fish dinner for the dogs. They all ate and drank a good amount. I walked around and stretched a bit and practiced resting in my sled for a couple hours. After a 6-hour rest, I hooked the team back up, pulled the snow hook and we were off.

A snow hook has two curved parallel prongs with a handle welded to the top of the prongs. A musher lifts the snow hook off the back of their sled and stomps on it with their foot to secure it deep into the snow. A rope is attached to the snow hook and extends to the front of the sled where it is securely attached to the towline. Once the musher stops the team by stepping on the claw break, attached to the bottom back of the sled, the snow hook is then secured into the snow like a boat anchor, to keep the dog team stopped. A musher can then safely snack the dogs or make some other needed adjustment in the team.

We departed White Mountain at 8 a.m. Dogs have an incredible sense of direction and knew they were going home. In about a month, I hoped to be at this same place, covering the last 77 miles of the Iditarod race. In three hours we arrived at the Topkot shelter cabin at the base of Topkot Mountain. I didn't want to push my luck, so I decided to shut them down for two hours. I immediately snacked the dogs and spent some time massaging each one. They all started laying down so I went inside and took an hour nap on a bunk. After this conservative rest stop, we were on our way again. The team continued to move at a rapid pace. We arrived back at our home at 6 p.m. with all dogs pulling strong in harness. I was elated and now confident that the team was ready.

I had taken my new reinforced toboggan sled on the training run to White Mountain. I was very pleased with how it had handled. I brought the sled into the house one evening to tighten all the bolts and to install a 6 by 24 inch piece of snow machine track with a bungee cord, for an extra brake. By stepping on this piece of track, I could easily slow the team down to a slower pace if necessary. The dogs would usually pick up speed when they would see any kind of movement. This piece of track was a necessary for keeping the team at a conservative pace.

The last two weeks we ran short 10-mile fun runs every other day that were designed to build moral and maintain muscle tone. Toenails were trimmed and the late Doc Leedy, our local vet, came out to our dog lot to give the 17 dogs their required medical exams and sign the required paperwork for the Iditarod Trail Committee. Earlier that month they had already been treated for worms and kennel cough for extra safe measures.

Ten days before leaving for the race, the basketball team and I traveled to Fairbanks to compete in the 3A-state tournament. To say Fairbanks is cold in the winter is a bit of an understatement. I found an out-fitter store that had cold weather clothing for outdoor recreation. I purchased some wind pants, mitts and a heavy-duty pullover wind parka for the race. Arriving home from Fairbanks, Penny sewed a wolverine ruff around the hood of it. The wolverine ruff keeps a mush-er's face warmer and does not allow condensation ice from breathing, to form in the extreme cold. She also made some warm fleece neck warmers that I could pull up over my nose when needed.

CHAPTER 3

OFF TO ANCHORAGE

"I named my kennel 'Dog-Gone-Happy-Kennels' because I wanted the experience of dog mushing to be as much fun for the dogs as it was for me."

Bill Jack – An Iditarod Dreamer

All the hard work and preparation had been exhausting. The anticipation of the unknown and all the horror stories of the trail I had heard over the years were causing me great anxiety. I kept trying to convince myself that everything would go smoothly, but knew the chances of that happening for a rookie would be unheard of. I have urged my children and students to always be the best they can be in whatever they attempt. I was now feeling the pressure of being the example. I wanted to enjoy the adventure, but at the same time, be somewhat competitive. The Iditarod trail can be unpredictable and I knew I would be required to make the best of many unexpected situations.

I was nervous as I prepared to leave for Anchorage. The race would begin on Saturday, but an all-day rookie meeting would be held on Tuesday. On Monday, Penny and I loaded 17 dogs into an Alaska Airlines igloo, designed with compartments for dogs to rest in. Harnesses, dog food, sleds and all the required gear, were also loaded.

Once a few rows of seats were taken off the 737 jet, the large igloo was shaped to snugly fit in the front of the passenger section of the aircraft through a huge front door that lifts upward. Once the igloo was fork lifted up and slid into the aircraft, it was then pushed back on installed rollers to make room for another igloo. Seats could be removed from these 737-200 aircrafts for either two igloos, leaving room for 72 passenger seats in the rear of the aircraft, or five igloos, leaving room for 26 seats. A wall panel separated the secured igloos from the passenger section. The jet was called the 737-200 combi. They were used for many years from Anchorage to remote Alaska. Since there were no roads to many of these towns, air travel played a huge role in shipping needed supplies and freight to these remote locations.

This flight had two igloos in the front, one being ours. After the ramp crew had loaded the igloos, I along with many other passengers boarded the aircraft up portable stairs through the rear of the aircraft. Alaska Airlines was a large sponsor of the Iditarod back then and gave mushers significant discounts for sending their dog teams to Anchorage, especially when many of the igloos were going back to Anchorage empty.

Our friends, Mark and Penny LaChapell were our Anchorage hosts that we hadn't seen for a few years. Mark was waiting for me at the airport and we drove over to the freight office to pick up the dog team. We loaded them, the sleds and all the gear into his truck. After we secured all the dogs in the truck, we were able to put all of the gear into the side panels. Finally the two sleds went on top of the truck's bed frame. What a load!

It was pouring down rain on the 25-mile trip to Mark's place in Peters Creek. We hurriedly strung out a 40-foot cable line between two birch trees. It was a quiet area parallel to his long driveway, a perfect place for the dogs to rest after their long unfamiliar trip. We unloaded the dogs, secured them along the cable and gave each one a large piece of frozen fish. It was midnight when we finished.

The next morning (Tuesday), I was up at 7 a.m. checking on the dogs. Mark loaned me one of his cars to drive to Wasilla for the all-day rookie meeting. This meeting was designed to help prepare rookies for their first Iditarod. There were 30 rookies signed up for the 1991 race, which was more than normal. After arriving at the Iditarod Headquarters, I found many of the mushers wandering around the museum-like facility, admiring the many pictures and displays of past Iditarods. Many tourists and school classes visit this facility every year. There were many shirts, books and other memorabilia for sale.

Once the meeting started, the Iditarod staff was introduced and then each rookie was asked to say a few words about themselves. Jack Niggemyer, the race manager, directed most of the meeting. During lunch, which was provided, and during breaks, the nervousness among the rookies seemed to ease as we visited with one another.

Mushers were reminded that very seldom does a rookie finish in the top 30. Much emphasis was placed on pacing your team, rest stops and the proper dog care necessary to just finish the race. Difficult sections of the trail were discussed and what we could do to travel through those areas successfully. We were reminded of the importance of being cordial to checkers, spectators, villagers and race officials especially if we were grumpy from the lack of sleep. The race manager concluded the day by encouraging us to stay positive and enjoy the magnificent country that we would be passing through.

On Wednesday, Mark and I ran the dogs for a few miles for the last time before the race. After cooking and feeding the team their dinner, I spent a good amount of time rubbing each dog down and giving them lots of attention. It was a needed restful day for me.

All day Thursday was a required meeting for all mushers at the Clarion Hotel (The Anchorage Iditarod Headquarters), near Lake Hood and the Anchorage International Airport. The race manager and race mar-shal were introduced and for hours, thoroughly explained the race rules. Iditarod was allowing a handler to ride a second sled for the first 35 miles to the Knik checkpoint, through the heavy spectator areas. Instructions were also given for the official Anchorage start on Saturday.

Penny and Thurman arrived in Anchorage that afternoon. We met in the lobby of the hotel shortly after the meeting. Thurman had been an incredible help the past three months. His reward was this trip to Anchorage. He and Elliot (Mark and Penny's 14 year old son) were now my dog handlers for the Iditarod start and had official armbands to prove it.

All the mushers and the media were concerned about the unusually warm temperatures; however, the forecast was calling for gradual cooling over the next few days. At least it had stopped raining. Thursday evening was the drawing banquet in downtown Anchorage. We were assigned to round-table 49. Norman Vaughan, who had finished his fourth Iditarod the previous year at age 84, gave a thought provoking invocation, asking God to watch over and protect each team. Vaughan was an Alaskan adventurer who had also accompanied Admiral Byrd to the South Pole in 1928. He had a very colorful history and was admired by all Alaskans. There was also a surprise tribute to Joe Redington Sr., who was running his 17th Iditarod this particular year at age 74. He was given the Spirit of the Iditarod Award. The halibut dinner was excellent and the atmosphere was festive. It was an exciting evening and Penny and I felt a little overwhelmed about being a part of it all.

Finally it was time to draw for starting positions. The first musher would leave the starting chute at 9 a.m. on Saturday. Every two minutes another musher would be released. There were 75 mushers this particular year. I was the 66th musher to sign up for the race so I was the 66th musher to draw. I drew number 49 to match the table we were sitting at and the number in the advertised length of the race (1049). I wondered if this meant I would be finishing in 49th place.

On Friday, which is called Iditarod Eve, Penny, Thurman and I drove to Anchorage to purchase some last minute items like warm socks, gloves for cooking, Gatorade mix and a variety of my snacks for the race. Early that evening, Thurman and Elliot went to a movie, while our hosts took Penny and I out for steak dinners at Club Paris in Anchorage. We had a great time laughing and enjoying our time together.

To be able to get to our designated holding area Saturday morning, we had to wake at 5 a.m. I tossed and turned most of the night, too anxious to sleep. The last hour in bed, I tried to just lay still. Finally it was time to get up and we were soon sipping coffee. We methodically reminded each other of everything that needed to be done. We were required to be at our assigned area in downtown Anchorage at 7 a.m. for our 10:30 a.m. scheduled departure.

Once we arrived, we found it to be very organized. We were directed to our parking spot, unloaded the dogs and secured them around the truck inside the fenced area. Penny and I would occasionally talk to the dogs, assuring them that everything was OK. This was all new for them, but they seemed to enjoy all the attention they were getting.

Wooden slat fences were everywhere that blocked off many streets and separated the sidewalks from the street where all the dog trucks and trailers were parked. Crowds of spectators were moving up and down the sidewalk taking pictures and wishing mushers the best of luck. At the starting line there were media platforms, loud speakers and television crews. The excitement was everywhere and all the activity was a little overwhelming.

Two hours before our start, Penny and I headed over to a restaurant to sit down and be alone. Mark, his wife, Thurman and Elliott watched over the dogs for us. The past three months had been an exhausting whirlwind and I needed a few minutes to stop and ask, "is this really happening?" We were here because four months ago, Penny had insisted that this was the year to do the Iditarod. It was a dream come true and Penny's vision got us here. This little pause helped settle my nerves.

Finally it was time to hook up the team. The dogs immediately became excited as we put on their harnesses. This alerted them that we would soon be doing what they love to do. I led Cheetah and Joe to the front of the tow-line and snapped the tug lines to their harnesses. They were my most dependable leaders. Cheetah and Joe were both born in our dog lot. Cheetah was now seven years old and Joe was four. They both loved being in front. Cheetah was a small black and white, blue-eyed beauty. Two months after being born, Cheetah demonstrated that she was the fastest dog in the litter. That's how she got her name.

After a couple years, Cheetah's littermate Daisy, was bred by a dog-named Ferlin, who belonged to Joe Runyan (the 1989 Iditarod champion). Our dog Joe came from that breeding. I guess that meant that Cheetah was Joe's 'aunt.' Joe turned into a 50-pound dog with a perfect build. Like Joe's 'Father' Ferlin, Joe was a powerful puller in lead, even through deep snow. He was named after

Joe Runyan. My oldest son, Joe, was also an indication of how I liked the name.

I was a little nervous about running this long string of 17 dogs through the streets of Anchorage. There were some long tunnels on the bike path that Cheetah and Joe would have to lead us through. They were around the second and third mile of the race that went under the New Seward Highway and Lake Otis Parkway. This would be a new experience for the dog team. I reminded myself, "relax, everything will be fine."

CHAPTER 4

ANCHORAGE TO SKWENTNA

"I'm convinced there is no more noble creature on earth than a good sled dog doing what it loves best."

Rick Armstrong – An Iditarod Finisher

Handlers were spread out holding the towline as we started moving my team in position, behind teams numbered 47 and 48. Penny was leading Cheetah and Joe by holding on to Joe's harness. Thurman and I were on the brakes of both sleds. People were three deep on both sides of 4th Avenue, for as far as I could see. My name was now being announced on the speaker system as my team moved into the starting position. Information about Penny, our kennel, and my expectations were broadcast all over the downtown area.

Thurman ran to the front to comfort Cheetah and Joe, while Penny quickly moved back to ride the second sled as my handler. I went up to the front of the team, knelt down and reassured Cheetah and Joe by scratching their necks. As I headed back to my sled, the dogs were lunging to go. Shortly after I arrived back to the first sled, the starter shouted out, "three, two, one," and we were off. I turned around and noticed Penny had a big smile, waving to the crowds as we quickly moved down 4th Avenue. She was enjoying this special ride as much as I. We had worked so hard together to make this happen. I almost didn't believe it was real.

Mushing this powerful team through the first 35 miles of populated areas, many potential problems with traffic, spectators or an encounter with a moose could happen. The long string of rested dogs were especially eager to go in the beginning of the race. Penny was helping me to brake and navigate through these areas. If there was a tangle up, she could run up and untangle, while I kept the team stopped with my brake.

The temperature was around 25 degrees Fahrenheit and it was a beautiful day. The city crews had done an excellent job, grooming snow down the middle of 4th Avenue and then down Cordova Street. At the end of Cordova Street (about one mile into the race), was a steep hill, (A popular area for spectators). The trail stakes then led us to the Chester Creek bike trail.

Cheetah and Joe led the team right through the tunnels like they had been there before. For miles, there were hundreds of people cheering and lining both sides of the snow covered trail. All the commotion seemed to spur the team on. The Anchorage newspaper on Friday had published the pictures of each musher with their starting number next to their name. Many spectators would match the musher's large number he or she was wearing to the newspaper identification and would offer encouragement by shouting our names as we went by. Immediately after crossing the bridge over Northern Lights Boulevard, the team moved nicely around a sharp curve. This was another popular place for spectators, since there was a large parking lot nearby at Goose Lake.

The Iditarod race manager directs three snow machines to stay one day ahead of the leaders all the way to Nome. They would put trail stakes in the snow every couple hundred of feet. A florescent strip of paint at the top is easily seen during the day. A reflector is also attached to the top of the stake, which mushers can easily see at night with their headlamps. The trailblazers may also reroute the trail around open water or other such hazards. They had challenges waiting for them as well.

After about a mile of wooded area between Northern Lights and Tudor Road, we came to our first road crossing. Police were at Tudor, stopping traffic whenever a musher approached. After crossing Tudor, it was about a ten-mile stretch on a trail that paralleled the Glenn Highway to the Eagle River checkpoint. The team moved along nicely with all the dogs in a conservative trot for the first 20 miles.

We arrived into the Eagle River Checkpoint and I was relieved that we had avoided any mishaps. The checker recorded the time and the next restart would occur in Wasilla (30 miles North) in exactly four hours from our arrival time in Eagle River. Between Eagle River and Wasilla was a four-lane highway. This 30-mile stretch was skipped because it was unsafe for dog teams.

I had arranged for Mark to meet us with his truck in Eagle River. After arriving, we loaded the dogs and sleds in Mark's pickup and headed to Mark and Penny's home to rest and snack the dogs in a quiet setting for about two hours. After the break, we loaded the dogs again and continued to the restart in Wasilla. Once there, our dogs were unloaded for the last time and secured around Mark's truck to wait for our second departure time.

Penny and I continued massaging and giving each dog plenty of attention. Finally our four hours were up and it was time for another count down. Thurman, Elliot, Mark and his wife Penny, helped move the team to the starting line. Penny and I were standing on our brakes. The dogs started lunging and it became difficult keeping the dogs from moving forward at the starting line.

Finally we were released. Penny and I remained on our brakes as the dogs sprinted through the starting chute. Police stopped traffic as we crossed the Parks Highway and then zipped on and across Lucille Lake. The Iditarod stakes then led us to the Knik Goose Bay Road. We slowed the team to a trot as we followed the ATV trail along the side the road for the next 12 miles. Many spectators in cars were traveling along the road, watching the teams progressing toward the Knik checkpoint. The movement of the cars excited the dogs, but the team was in sync, maintaining a fast smooth trot.

We arrived in Knik around 7:30 p.m. Penny had ridden the second sled up to this third checkpoint. It had been a very long day, but we had really enjoyed mushing together for the first 35 miles of the race. Mark was waiting for us at Knik and helped unhook the second sled. It was now dark out. Knik is where the dog teams leave the crowds. Mushers checked in, gave hugs and kisses to loved ones and were off. I was experiencing a lot of mixed emotions. It was time to say thank you and goodbye to everyone. In addition, I was experiencing a lot of anxiety about the unknown that lay ahead.

Penny reminded me, "it's a long way to Nome." She continued, "I don't know whether to laugh or cry." The preparation the past three months had drained us both. At the same time, I think she was relieved to finally release me into the wild. We gave each other a farewell kiss and a bear hug. The dogs were lunging. I turned my headlamp on, pulled the snow hook and we quickly disappeared into the dark night.

This flat section of trail was about 85 miles to Skwentna. The first four hours was a bumpy ride with trees lining both sides of the trail. There were some open areas where spectators had ridden their snow machines to watch us pass by. Several of these areas were lit up with people gathered around campfires.

After four hours, my team passed Flathorn Lake, and I decided to shut the team down and take a four-hour rest. It had been a stressful day for the dogs and myself. This was 1991. Today's (2020) Iditarod race, and since around 2003, the Iditarod starts with an easy 10-mile ceremonial start through Anchorage to a staging area in a secluded area near the BLM (Bureau of Land Management) airstrip. The next day, mushers drive their teams in trucks to Willow (60 miles North of Anchorage). This is where the official Iditarod race starts at 2 p.m. on the first Sunday of March every year. Mushers and dogs get a good night's rest. The start of the race today (2020), is much less stressful for the dogs and mushers then it was in 1991.

Since leaving Anchorage, we had traveled approximately 70 miles. Rest stops can vary, but rest stops usually equal the run times. If I ran my team for eight hours, I planned on resting them for eight hours. Each musher has their own run/rest schedule that is best for their dogs.

We pulled off the trail about 30 feet and I unhooked each dog's neckline so they could maneuver to their choice of a resting spot. I immediately gave each dog a frozen fish snack. I then poured 12 ounces of Heet fuel into the insulation in the pie pan at the bottom of my cooker and lit a match to it. I placed my three-gallon pot into my cooker and started adding snow to the pot. Melting snow in my cooker took a long time, but eventually I had a pot of boiling water. The 12 ounces of liquid Heet that created a hot blue flame lasted about 40 minutes, especially if the hinged top of the cooker was closed.

Most all checkpoints had water. It only took about 15 minutes for water to boil in my cooker when water was available. When I had to melt snow, it took over 40 minutes to get a pot of water to boil. I should have put some hot water in my cooler before leaving Mark's home. This would have significantly shortened my cooking time and given me some time to rest in my sled. This was my first of many rookie mistakes.

Once the water was boiling, I poured the hot water over a good amount of cut up frozen fish in my three-gallon cooler. I added some high protein Iams commercial dog food and mixed up the teams' dinner. Each dog eagerly ate a full dish of fish soup. Every so often a team would quietly pass by.

The next section of trail would be a long stretch on the Yetna and Skwentna Rivers. Before leaving, I put booties on my dogs' feet for the first time. At the musher meeting on Thursday, we were told that the river ice conditions would probably require booties. For me, this meant 30 minutes of cold hands and backbreaking work.

The booties would protect the dogs' paws from the abrasive ice conditions. Snow can also be chewed up like sugar by snow machines. This condition also required booties because the sugar snow can get packed in between a dog's paw and create irritating cracks. The cracks require massaging in some ointment that contains zinc oxide, which helps to promote healing. I had purchased my booties at a specialty store for dog mushers in Anchorage. They were made out of a sturdy fleece material that lasted for about 40 to 50 miles.

Booties are fastened by a strip of Velcro sewn into the top of a bootie. If the Velcro is fastened to tight, the dog's circulation is restricted. If it is fastened to loose, it will soon come off. It took me a while to learn the proper feel when fastening the Velcro. Race rules require a musher to always carry a bag of booties for your team. An Iditarod musher may use around 1,000 booties during the race. They simply are used to prevent paw problems.

After a much needed four-hour rest for the dogs, we departed the rest area. The team moved up the Yetna and Skwentna Rivers at a very nice clip. I kept the team in a quick but conservative trot. I knew from running cross-country in high school and many marathons as an adult, how important pacing was to maintain a conservative speed. After mushing dogs for eight years, I was convinced that this principle applied to sled dogs as well. In recent years, I have noticed mushers Jeff King, Ramey Smyth and Mitch Seavey, demonstrating this principle. Their teams as a result, displayed faster times the last three hundred miles of the race.

The morning light gradually appeared and I was relieved to have survived my first night on the Iditarod. We arrived at the Skwentna checkpoint at 10 a.m. The checkpoint was on the snow covered river. Most of the leaders in the race were still there.

The Skwentna checkpoint was maintained by Joe and Norma Delia. Their home was up on the riverbank and they welcomed mushers in to rest and visit. Joe had me sign in and led me to a nice spot near the riverbank. After unhooking each neckline, I distributed straw (Provided by the Iditarod), for each dog. I then took each dog's booties off and checked their feet. I gave them a quick snack and decided to rest the team for eight hours. I had only slept for about four hours the past 48, so I headed to the Delia home to rest and warm up.

After a good one-hour sleep, I felt much better. I headed back to my dog team and found them all curled up and sleeping. Hot water was available here in a 55-gallon drum that was continuously filled by volunteers. This would dramatically cut my cooking time. When the veterinarian came by to examine my team, I led him to one of my dogs named Cubby. He had somehow poked his eye into the cable line at Mark's place. I had taken him to a local vet and he had advised me to watch his performance closely. I could tell Cubby was not feeling well. The vet and I both felt dropping Cubby was in his best interests. I left the required paperwork with the vet and the person in charge of dropped dogs. I also left plenty of dog food for Cubby.

There is a volunteer person at every checkpoint who is solely responsible for taking care of dropped dogs. To identify the musher that a dog belongs to, a tag is attached to the dog's collar before the race ever starts. Cubby would be carefully taken care and eventually flown back to his home in Nome. Today (2020), dogs in the race have a chip implanted under its skin that identifies their musher.

Volunteer veterinarians come to the Iditarod from all over the world and are carefully spread out over several checkpoints. Vets check teams when they enter a checkpoint. As the dog teams move up the trail, the vets take turns leapfrogging by airplane to a checkpoint ahead of the race. A vet logbook is required gear for Iditarod mushers. If the logbook or any required gear is lost, it may mean disqualification. Gear checks may occur at any checkpoint.

I found it very difficult to sit there in Skwentna and watch teams depart all day. I kept telling myself that this extra rest would pay off later down the trail. It also allowed my team to rest during the heat of the day. The dogs run much faster at night, because of the drop in temperature. Some people think they run faster at night because of the wolf instinct they possess in their DNA.

Joe Redington Sr. pulled in right behind me and declared his 24-hour. The race rules require a musher to take one 24-hour rest at any checkpoint of their choice. A musher must declare it when he or she checks in, however, they may change their mind and declare it at another checkpoint down the trail. Running the Iditarod requires mushers to be flexible and to keep their options open. Knowing the weather forecasts can help a musher's decision to know when it is best to leave a checkpoint. Iditarod checkers usually have forecast updates.

It takes about an hour to organize snacks for the next stretch of the trail, repack the sled and bootie all the dogs. After eight hours of rest in the heat of the day, I departed Skwentna with 16 dogs at 6 p.m.

CHAPTER 5

SKWENTNA TO ROHN

"It's a long way from Anchorage to Nome. Now I
know why they invented airplanes."

Bert Hanson – Iditarod Air Force Pilot

Leaving Skwentna, dog teams start entering the foothills
of the Alaska Range. Mount Denali, at 20,308 feet,
North America's highest peak, is in this rugged range of
mountains. Happy River Canyon is a challenge to cross
through, the weather can be fierce going over Rainy Pass
and the Delzell Gorge can be dangerous to maneuver a
dog team through. The Alaska Range has large trees most
everywhere. I was little nervous about mushing through
the next 100 miles of this rugged mountain terrain.

It took five hours to move from Skwentna to the
Finger Lake checkpoint. Living in Nome where the
countryside is wide open, I had never mushed through
such wooded trails. The ups and downs, quick turns

and maneuvering around trees with the heavy sled was extremely taxing on my upper body. There was no problem staying awake traveling through this part of the trail. My dogs seemed to perk up and enjoy the new experience.

The team was performing nicely. This made me feel good, but I kept reminding myself what Penny had said to me back in Knik, "it is a long way to Nome." I paid a great deal of attention to Cheetah and Joe, who were leading, realizing my team would only keep going as long as they did. Good leaders are hard to find. Cheetah and Joe were exceptional and had performed well in many races for me the past two years. I had a tremendous amount of confidence in the two of them, but they had never done the Iditarod, known as 'The Last Great Race On Earth.'

I pulled into Finger Lake at 11 p.m. The next section to Rainy Pass included the steep dreaded 'steps' (As they are referred to) into Happy River Canyon. I did not want to go down these steps in the dark. That meant I would have to wait another eight hours before daylight. I decided if I had to be here for eight hours, I might as well take my 24-hour rest here. I declared my 24-hour as I checked in, knowing I could later change my mind.

After cooking and taking care of the dogs, I entered the tent that was set up for mushers. It was 3 a.m. I had only slept a couple hours over the past three days. I crawled into my sleeping bag and soundly slept for seven hours. It was 10 a.m. when I went out to check on the dogs and noticed heavy clouds had moved in. I immediately became afraid of a heavy snow falling in the mountains before I could get over Rainy Pass. I realized

I needed to leave Finger Lake and hopefully get over the pass before that happened.

I finally departed 12 hours after arriving at Finger Lake at 11 a.m. I was a little disgusted with myself having stayed there five more hours than I needed to. The dogs were well rested, but this long stretch meant getting through the Happy River Canyon, the exhausting climb over Rainy Pass and down the very challenging Delzell Gorge. Thank goodness, it was now daylight and that would help me get through the dreaded Happy River Canyon.

The Finger Lake checker had advised me that the Happy River drop-offs were about 10 miles ahead. As each mile went by, the anticipation became nerve racking. After about an hour, there was this steep little hill that took a sharp left turn at the bottom. Dog teams that had gone through here before me had made a trail 30 feet straight into the bushes. My leaders followed the sled marks and went straight into it before I could get the team stopped. I put my snow hooks in and hurried up to my leaders. By the time I had turned the team around and led them out of the deep snow, I was totally out of breath.

Continuing another half mile, I came to the first step. The trail was carved about 30 inches wide, 50 feet down the side of this huge bank. I slammed on my claw break that went deep into the snow, but going through this section of trail with 16 dogs was crazy. At the bottom of the first step, the trail curved around about a hundred yards on this plateau, to set up a dog team to go straight down step two. I stood on my claw brake with both feet as we zoomed down the steep narrow shelf.

The third and last step was the worst. There was a 60-degree blind corner leading into it. I slammed on my claw break, but instead of going deep into the snow, it came down on my snow machine track brake. As my sled flew off the ledge sideways, I jumped off my sled and ran down the narrow path. I watched the sled twist 360-degrees in midair. It landed on its side in the snow at the bottom. In the process the team had continued down the ledge. When the sled landed on its side in the deep snow, it helped stop the team. I was devastated, thinking my sled was beyond repair and my dream of running the Iditarod had come to a screeching halt.

Miraculously, I was relieved that the only damage was a slight crack in the handlebar. I spent about 10 minutes reinforcing it with some duct tape. The dogs were looking back at me like, why did we stop here. I felt very lucky and the dogs took off like nothing had happened. We continued 100 yards onto the Happy River. I decided to snack the team. I obviously needed the pause more than the dogs did. As I handed out snacks to each dog, I thanked God for watching over me and asked for His continued protection.

After crossing the river, the team muscled up a long steep climb out of the canyon. I wondered, as we moved along, if Happy River got its name because everyone seemed happy to have survived the steps. The trail eventually became kind and the team moved swiftly over the next 15 miles, arriving at the Rainy Pass checkpoint at 4 p.m. There were nine teams resting. I found my two food bags nearby. After opening them, I started snacking the dogs and reorganizing my sled. I packed four bags of snacks and a bag of booties into the sled. As the dogs rested, I continued to snack them about every 20 minutes. I left the remaining dog food that I didn't need, for the person in charge of dropped dogs.

Malcomb Vance, Roger Roberts and I, all pulled out together at 5:30 p.m. It was snowing and there was a strong wind causing low visibilities. It became difficult following the trail stakes. Our three teams took turns breaking trail. After three hours, we all stopped for a 20-minute break and snacked our dogs. The three of us shared some candy bars. I decided to put my older leader, Goosak, up front with Cheetah and give Joe a break.

Goosak was a seven-year old female that was also born in our dog lot. She was a very gentle, loving dog and the friendliest I ever had. Goosak was a fast steady leader that was very responsive to my voice commands. She was half Siberian husky. I named Goosak after a Russian fur trader named William Goosak. William had brought a team of Siberian huskies from Siberia to Nome in 1908 to run in the 1909 All Alaskan Sweepstakes sled dog race. This popular race was held every April for ten years from 1908 to 1917. It followed the telegraph line from Nome across the Seward Peninsula to the mining town of Candle and back to Nome for a total distance of 408 miles.

The Siberian husky team came in a surprising second place in 1909. A Nome musher named Fox Maule Ramsey was so impressed, he made a trip across the International Date Line to the Anadyr River area of Siberia during the summer of 1909 and brought back 60 more Siberian huskies. John "Iron Man" Johnson won the 1910 All Alaskan Sweepstakes with a team of Ramsey's Siberian huskies, setting a new record of just over 74 hours.

This race was the event of the year for the town of Nome. Updates were frequently telegraphed in from mining camp checkpoints to the race headquarters located at the Board of Trade Saloon. The robust minors loved to gamble and the betting was lively and spirited. The race abruptly ended during World War I when many of the men of Nome went to war. Our Goosak was most likely a descendent of those Siberian huskies from the Sweepstakes era.

In 1983, the Nome Kennel Club sponsored the 75th anniversary running of the All Alaskan Sweepstakes. Iditarod champion Rick Swenson won the winner-take-all, $25,000 purse. In 2008, the Nome Kennel Club again sponsored the 100th Anniversary running of the race and Iditarod champion Mitch Seavey won the winner-take-all, $100,000 prize money.

It was now dark as my team started the final 1200-foot ascent up Rainy Pass. Blowing snow had filled the trail with snow, which significantly slowed our progress. I frequently would get off the runners and walk alongside the sled to lighten the load. It was a slog, but finally reaching the highest peak in the race gave me a triumphant feeling.

We picked up speed as we descended down this massive one-mile long chute into the Delzell Gorge. Once in the gorge, the dogs became excited, zig-zagging around open water and across a few snow bridges. The snow machine trailblazers had made these bridges by placing large branches close together over the creek water and then shoveling snow over the top of the branches.

The trail sometimes went up one side of the ravine and then crossed to the other side. Thick bushes on the curvy trail made it impossible to see around many of the corners. The dogs were cruising down this gorge. My claw brake was not able to slow them down much. I kept complimenting my leaders who were both excellent at following my voice commands. 'Gee' meant go right, 'haw' meant go left and 'on by' meant keep going.

It was an incredible challenge maneuvering my sled around these corners and keeping it upright. I was very alert and attentive on this stretch of trail. This exhilarating ride went for miles and I was relieved to finally come out of the gorge onto the Tatina River without a mishap.

After about a mile on the river, we mushed into a quiet area with huge spruce trees that were everywhere. This was the Rohn checkpoint, a beautiful and wind protected refuge in the midst of the Alaska Range. It was several minutes after midnight as my team pulled up to the BLM shelter cabin. The Rohn checker had me sign in and I declared my 24-hour. A volunteer led my team about 100 feet to a quiet resting spot. Many teams were widely spread out and seemed to have their own secluded area among the trees.

I bedded the dogs down and rewarded each one with a quick snack. After about 15 minutes, the vet appeared and examined each dog. He reported to me, "their feet all look good, just make sure you feed them real good here on your 24-hour." They all curled up while I boiled water for their first meal here. I had sent extra food to this checkpoint, thinking I might take my 24-hour at Rohn. I mixed ground beef and Eukanuba dog food in my cooler, then poured three gallons of boiling water over the dog food. After stirring it all up, I filled each aluminum dog dish and carefully served each dog. Once a dog finished his meal, I would keep offering a little more. Some of the dogs wanted more than others. I was relieved to see them all eating enthusiastically.

The BLM cabin was for the checker and his staff. I felt very safe in this peaceful sanctuary and was relieved to have arrived. The Alaska Range was still all around us. This majestic mountain range made me feel like I was microscopic, as I was slowly, but progressively, moving through it. I stretched out and rested on the sled with my sleeping bag as a blanket. The dogs curled up and slept on their beds of straw. After a five-hour sleep, I was up at daybreak and boiling water for the dogs' next meal of salmon.

At the musher meeting before the race, I had talked to the University of Alaska Sports Medicine staff about how to avoid leg cramps that I often experienced. They suggested taking a couple swigs of pure maple syrup every day. They advised me that it is absorbed into the blood stream faster than say Gatorade. I had bought a flask and some real maple syrup before leaving Anchorage. Every 12 hours when I boiled water, I would toss the flask of maple syrup into the hot water for a bit and would then take a couple of swigs of it. It seemed to be working because I had not experienced any leg cramps.

The dogs ate well again and afterward, they went back to sleep. All day, teams were quietly arriving and departing, many having completed their 24-hour and others planning on taking theirs at Nikolai, McGrath or Takotna. It was difficult at this point in the race to get an idea of what place I was in. Maybe by Ophir, after everyone had taken their 24-hour rest, I would have a better idea.

Since I was taking my long rest in Rohn, this is where I would make up my differential (the difference in the official start times in Anchorage). I started in 49th place out of 75 mushers. That meant I would be here 52 minutes longer than 24 hours. The official checker told me I would be released at 1:02 a.m. The checkers have a huge role and responsibility to play, keeping track of all the times.

As the dogs rested, I checked my runners for smoothness. I used a metal track system that was screwed to the bottom of the wooden runners. I could quickly slide new Teflon runners onto the metal track if they needed replacing. The runners looked fine.

We rested and snacked all day long. I fed the dogs their last hot meal at 9 p.m., four hours before our departure time. It was now dark and it started to snow. Even though I could not feel the wind, I could hear it blowing in the tree tops 60 feet up. I shook as I imagined fierce winds blowing on the long 90-mile stretch to Nikolai. Rohn was beginning to feel too secure and I started to dread leaving the protection of this refuge. We rested two more hours.

At about 11 p.m., I felt chilled, so I drank a cup of hot Gatorade from my thermos and walked down to the checker's cabin to get warm. Eventually, I headed back to the team and started packing up. I placed new batteries in my headlamp and made sure my spare headlamp was in good working order. I put two sets of dry socks on and switched my caribou fur mukluks to my bunny boots. Bunny boots are well-insulated boots that were issued by the military to recruits in cold climates.

My thermos bottle was filled with hot Gatorade. I placed it and plenty of snacks in a pouch attached to the back of the sled where I could easily reach, when mushing down the trail. I packed several bags of fish, lamb and ground beef for the dogs' snack breaks that I would give every few hours. I put booties on all 16 dogs. I was released at 1:02 a.m.

CHAPTER 6

ROHN TO OPHIR

"Running and caring for sled dogs out on the trail and at checkpoints is a full time job with little rest for the musher."

Lavon Barve – Multi Top Ten Finisher

The 16 rested dogs tore out of the wooded refuge onto the river's glare ice (slippery frozen ice with no snow covering). I stood on both brakes with all my weight, but it didn't help much as we zipped down the river about 15 mph. With very little control, it was a crazy, frightening ride. A half-mile down the icy river, the trail took a sharp left turn into the woods. Cheetah and Joe were trying to make the turn as I was yelling "haw, haw, haw," but it was too slippery and instead of following the trail into the woods, we went into thick brush and stopped. I quickly ran up and was finally able to lead Cheetah and Joe back on the snow packed trail, where the braking action would be good.

For the next three hours we were challenged, maneuvering through the western foothills of the Alaska Range. There were plenty of ups and downs, sharp turns and trees everywhere. Climbing to the top of a very steep hill, we came across some slippery spring water ice. Cheetah with her booties on, slipped on the ice and my swing dog Foxy, caught up to her and a fight started.

I quickly set my snow hooks into the snow and ran up to break it up. Foxy ended up with a puncture wound in his leg and Cheetah had a puncture wound on her face. I moved Foxy farther back in the team and brought Goosak up to the swing position behind Cheetah. Those two got along really well. I then packed their puncture wounds with triple antibiotic cream and decided to continue administering the ointment at snack breaks.

Cheetah was definitely the dominant dog in the team. She always wanted to be in the lead. When Foxy caught up to her, she thought that he was trying to take over the lead position. She didn't like that and was trying to let Foxy know who was boss. Sometimes there are personality conflicts in the team. I found that two females or two males are more likely to fight with one another. I usually had a male running next to a female. That simply eliminated a lot of potential conflicts.

The trail continued to be exhausting. There were long stretches where the trail had a side slant to it, with big trees on the down side edge of the trail. It would take all my might to make the heavy sled miss a tree, but every two or three trees I would miss, the sled would slam into another. This went on for miles and with a fresh 16 dogs raring to go, the sled and I took a beating.

After about two hours of this, I came to a small clearing where musher Kazuo Kogima from Japan had stopped to fix his broken sled. He was using his long handled axe and some duct tape to replace one of the main back supports of his sled. I felt lucky that my sled was still in good shape. It was a stretch where all mushers' sleds would have been tested for strength. He took off and I decided this was a good spot to take a snack break for the dogs.

Ahead were many long lakes with glare ice. Luckily it was getting light, but it was still very difficult following sled marks over these icy lakes. Cheetah and Joe did an exceptional job leading us across and following my gee/ haw commands. The Farewell Burn was next. It consisted of miles of burnt stubby spruce trees from a long-ago forest fire. There was sufficient snow cover and the trail became straight as an arrow. We stopped for another snack at 8 a.m.

As we moved down the trail, I suddenly noticed a cow (Female) moose and her yearling calf, running parallel with my team. They were about 100 yards off to our left. The dogs became excited and started loping (Similar to a gallop). I decided to let the team lope as long as my leaders stayed on the trail. After about a half-mile, we had outrun the moose so I slowed the team down to a conservative trot.

The countryside was quite barren at this point. There was no wind, the trail was nicely packed, the clouds were blocking the sun and I was hoping to make some good time. The visibility was excellent. I frequently turned and enjoyed the view of the massive Alaska Range that we had successfully passed through.

Around noon, I passed four teams who had pulled off the trail and were resting. I estimated we had about 30 miles to go. My team was still moving at a nice clip, so I decided to continue to mush on into Nikolai. I arrived at 3 p.m. and the checker informed me that he would be doing a required gear check. This happens at two or three unannounced checkpoints during the race and at the finish line as well. I opened up my sled bag and pointed out the snowshoes, sleeping bag, a bag of dog booties, my promotional material, my vet notebook, my cooker, extra dog food and my ax. He then allowed me to sign in and I was led to my rest area.

I bedded the dogs down and cooked a hot meal for them. Their endurance was beginning to surprise me. I had no idea that they could finish the last 30 miles of a 90-mile run so efficiently. I planned a long rest here. I was assigned a home in Nicolai and was able to call Penny collect for the first time. Hearing her voice was emotional. I choked-up as she immediately wanted to know how things were going. Too much had happened to share, but she was relieved to hear how far I had come and that everything was OK. She informed me that every day, Thurman, Mori and Dana were excited to check on their Dad. She continued, "We go down to the Nome Iditarod Race Headquarters and observe your checkpoint arrival times." She encouraged me by saying, "we are rooting for you." I missed them all.

In the 1991 Iditarod, a musher's arrival time was phoned in to Anchorage or Nome by village checkers. In the remote areas on the trail, updates were transmitted by shortwave ham radio operators. Computer printouts were on bulletin boards at the Nome and Anchorage Iditarod Headquarters. The updates were eventually posted online. Since then, the technology has advanced to instant communication.

Today (2020), Iditarod mushers carry a position locator. People around the world, via satellite, can go to Iditarod.com and by joining the 'Insider' for a small fee, can immediately follow each musher down the trail. In addition, the Insider crew physically follows the race out on the trail by airplane. Every day they post musher interviews, live updates and incredible scenic videos. My favorite videos to watch are the, 'Run Dogs Run' videos.

After a nine-hour rest, we left Nikolai at midnight for a 50-mile mush to McGrath. The team was a little sluggish, but after a while, they picked up the pace. This was the norm. After the dogs had eaten and rested at a checkpoint, each dog for the first half hour of the run would slow the team a bit as they took turns squatting to relieve themselves on the run. Most of this run was on the Kuskokwim River. The temperature had dropped to -40 degrees Fahrenheit and the dogs were moving nicely.

We arrived in McGrath at 6 a.m. On the run to McGrath, I noticed three of my dogs were slightly limping. After arriving, the vet determined that all three had shoulder injuries. I suspected they sustained these injuries over the Delzell Gorge or somewhere on the brutal three-hour section out of Rohn. I decided to drop all three dogs in McGrath.

I loaded my two bags of dog food on my sled and mushed my team down the street to Jerry and Sherrell Holtzhouser's home. They are good friends of ours. Jerry worked for the National Weather Service in McGrath. I planned a 12-hour rest, so I bedded the dogs down on straw, gave each dog a frozen hunk of lamb and would cook for them later. I went inside and Sherrell quickly suggested I take a hot shower. I must have smelled pretty bad. During my shower, Sherrell had made me a hearty breakfast of pancakes, sausage, eggs and coffee.

After talking and catching up, she led me to a spare bedroom with a very comfortable bed. I passed out for four hours. On the Iditarod, conditions can be so miserable one hour and extremely the opposite the next. Mood swings can be steep and swift. Sleep was one of those factors that lifted my spirit dramatically.

I spent much time that afternoon, complimenting the dogs as I cooked for them. Their appetites continued to be fantastic. I gave the dogs a lot of attention by talking to each one as I massaged their legs, hips and shoulder muscles. Since I was now down to 13 dogs, it would be a more manageable number.

I mentioned to Sherrell that being out in the elements 24/7, it was difficult staying hydrated. She immediately handed me a cold Pepsi and then made me a sandwich to go with it. I told Sherrell that having some food other than granola and trail mix was much appreciated. Before leaving, Jerry took out his guitar and sang a couple of songs for me with his two boys sitting next to him. It had been an enjoyable 12-hour rest stop.

The 1991 race was the last year a musher could stay and be taken care of in someone's home at a checkpoint. Starting in 1992, mushers were required to stay in a corral like setting at a checkpoint. This rule is still in effect today. The reason was because a few mushers had organized a network of people's homes to rest at. This gave those few mushers a huge advantage over other mushers who didn't have the time to organize such a restful pattern. This new rule of corralling was meant to help level the playing field.

I departed McGrath at 6 p.m. It was a three-hour mush to Takotna. I had heard a lot about the hospitality that this gold mining town of about 50 residents provided the Iditarod mushers. After arriving, they invited me into the community hall for a turkey dinner and home-made pie. The town people worked in shifts preparing food and making mushers feel at home. It was a festive atmosphere. Musher Roger Roberts was there. I had seen Roger in Finger Lake. We had also traveled through a snowstorm, taking turns breaking trail over Rainy Pass. We had also both taken our 24-hour in Rohn.

Shortly after finishing our incredible meals, I followed Roger out of Takotna. Roger had lived in Nome for the past few years, but had spent a lot of time around Takotna working some gold mining claims. This section had some rolling hills, but the trail was good. Our teams were moving at the same speed and I was careful to keep my team about 200 feet back from his so my team wouldn't distract his dogs.

We arrived at 1 a.m. and were ushered into a nice parking spot out of the wind near the cabin. There was water in pails, ready for mushers to use. The fuel and food drops were nearby and the area had a lot of trees that protected the rest areas from the wind. Dick Forsgren owns the only cabin in Ophir and he opens it up each year for the Iditarod. The cabin was warm and a welcome spot for rest.

It had been a 60-mile trip to Ophir from McGrath. The next section was a very remote 90-mile run to the old mining area of Iditarod. I planned to run straight through to Iditarod so I decided to rest my dogs for 12 hours. Inside the cabin, Rick Armstrong advised me we were in about 45th and 46th positions. That meant there were 30 teams behind us. This was the first time in the race that I really knew what place I was in. Rick had run the Iditarod before and knew a great deal about pacing. He seemed to think we were in good position to still place in the top 25 finishers.

I was a little surprised at his prediction, but listened with interest. I had helped Rick in Rainy Pass and had given him some wire that he needed to repair his sled. Again in Rohn, he needed more wire. I figured that I probably wouldn't need it so I had given him the whole roll. The musher from Japan and Rick's problems with his broken sled, led me to believe that there were many teams that had broken sleds to repair.

Rick advised me that there was no rush to leave this checkpoint. He explained that the next 160 miles to Shageluk through Iditarod, is never used during the winter and the trail would be soft. He said that by traveling over this trail a day after the leaders, gave the trail a chance to set up and harden. It would be much faster for us and much easier on the dogs. I was wondering why Rick was giving me all this valuable information. Maybe he was showing some appreciation for all the wire I had given him! Regardless, I was thankful. I gave the dogs a couple good meals here and was able to get a couple hours of sleep. I had sent some extra food here, knowing it would be a long 90-mile run to Iditarod.

CHAPTER 7

OPHIR TO KALTAG

"There is little on earth that can match the inner pride of succeeding in a battle with Mother Nature."

Stan Smith – Iditarod Finisher

On odd years, the southern route leaves Ophir and goes through Iditarod and Shageluk, then eventually to Anvik, the first village on the Yukon River. On even years, the northern route leaves Ophir and goes north through Cripple (A tent set-up checkpoint), to the village of Ruby, which is on the Yukon. Either way, once a musher reaches the mighty Yukon River, it is a 150-mile mush on the Yukon to the village of Kaltag. These two routes allow more villages to experience the excitement of the Iditarod. Considering the long history of the sled dogs in Bush Alaska, one village resident described it like this, "the Iditarod is like bringing the Super Bowl through our village."

After the 12-hour rest, I decided to pull out of Ophir behind Rick, at 1 p.m. His team at this point was much faster than mine and disappeared into the horizon. My team was moving slowly out of Ophir into the Beaver Mountains. After about two hours, I decided to shut the team down for an hour. After the break, it started to cool down and the team started gaining momentum.

At sunset, we were now heading south. About a half mile to the west, I noticed thousands of caribou grazing. The dogs smelled their presence and picked up their pace. It was a clear night and the temperature was dropping. After about two hours it was pitch black out. I turned my headlamp off and I could not even see my hand in front of my face. I immediately turned the headlamp back on.

An hour later, all the dog's heads snapped to the right but kept moving straight ahead. I turned my head to the right and my headlamp reflected off two sets of eyes looking toward me. It was spooky. Dogs at times, alert you to things that you would otherwise miss. I was hoping that those eyes were a couple moose and not a pack of wolves.

During snack breaks, I placed both snow hooks into the snow to positively secure the team. My temperature gage showed it was -42 degrees Fahrenheit. We were in one of the most remote areas of Alaska. I did not want to doze off and fall off my sled. Watching my team continue down the trail without me would be devastating. My every move became very deliberate.

At my next snack break, I dropped both snow hooks on each side of my sled and stepped on them to keep the team at a standstill. I went up to my leaders and snacked them first so they would keep the line taut. I then moved slowly back to the sled making sure each dog received a good share. I had not seen another musher for the past eight hours. I felt very alone. My dogs started barking. They wanted to go. I pulled both hooks and off we went. I kept looking back as I sensed something was chasing us. My imagination was performing well.

As we swiftly and silently continued across the snow for hours, I was in awe, watching the many falling stars throughout this moonless night. During the long stretch of trail, I was also treated to greenish glowing Northern Lights dancing across the sky. It was enchanting and created an emotional high. The dogs continued to move along at a fast clip. Their speed demonstrated to me that they were enjoying this magical night as much as I was.

I was very alone traveling between checkpoints. I was traveling across this magnificent country in complete silence that enhanced the experience. During these hours and hours of solitude, I found myself talking to God a lot more than I was used to. This particular night I was humbly thanking Him for the amazing display of the night sky I was experiencing. I continued thanking Him for the miracle of life and for my loving family. I asked Him to provide a shield of protection to surround each one. I thanked Him for this incredible adventure and for these special animals that were moving me across this vast land.

After 12 hours on this stretch of trail, I suddenly noticed a light about two miles ahead. The trail was a little blown in, but we seemed to move at a nice pace toward the light. When we reached it, I was surprised to find it to be a biker, struggling and walking his bike up a hill. I told Cheetah and Joe, "on by." As we passed, I stepped on my claw break and asked him if he was all right. He assured me he was fine and thought that the Iditarod checkpoint was only a couple miles ahead. As I continued down the trail, I asked myself, "did that really just happen or am I hallucinating."

The Iditarod Trail Invitational is the world's longest human powered foot, ski or bike ultra-marathon race. This race has also been known as the Iditasport. It starts a week before the Iditarod Sled Dog Race and follows the Iditarod Trail. The race goes from Knik to McGrath (350 miles) or from Knik to Nome (950 miles). It is an incredible challenge under extreme conditions and a few hearty souls compete every year. Rules have changed over the years and today (2020), a participant must have completed the section from Knik to McGrath to qualify to go all the way to Nome in a future race. Check out the interesting videos on the website: iditarodtrailinvitational.com.

Unfortunately, the biker's estimate was way off. Instead of a couple miles, it was more like 15 more miles. I arrived in Iditarod at 3 a.m. After taking care of my team, I took my warm sleeping bag into the large unheated musher's tent to get some sleep. I tossed and turned for a couple hours, but found it too cold to sleep. I guess I was afraid I would freeze to death if I blacked out.

I stayed busy all day cooking for the dogs, massaging their muscles and just moving around, trying to stay warm. I decided to drop two more dogs. The vet did not find anything wrong with them, but their performance the last 50 miles clearly showed me that they were no longer interested in pulling. I was now down to 11 dogs. I filled out the paperwork and left plenty of dog food for the person taking care of dropped dogs.

After 12 hours in Iditarod I headed for Shageluk at 3 p.m. This section was 65 miles in length and filled with lots of hills. The trail was a little blown in. I would help the dogs by running up the hills and then would jump on the runners going down.

About halfway there, the trail started following a high ridgeline. The visibility was endless in every direction. The sun was setting and the sky colors reflecting off the mountaintops were beautiful. The cold yellow rays of the sun started reflecting off the gentle blowing snow, giving it a translucent quality. The whole countryside was moving in a lemon-colored glow. Riding quietly along on the runners, the scene was breathtaking and a beauty beyond words. I thought about how God is such an incredible living artist. His colorful landscapes are everywhere. This experience made me more aware of the beauty in His creations. It was a confirmation that He is alive and well. I immediately thanked Him for the miracle of sight and the ability to be able to see it all in living color.

I finally arrived in Shageluk at 1 a.m. The checker led me a short distance to the school where a number of teams were parked. I found a quiet secluded spot and bedded the team down as I snacked them. I had not slept for two days and decided to go into the school and get some much-needed sleep. Unfortunately, I blacked out for seven hours.

There was a family of four that had flown in from California and chose Shageluk to experience the Iditarod this particular year. I thought they were mushers who were asleep when I came in during the middle of the night. In the morning, I answered their many questions. I soon explained that I had to get busy and cook for my dogs. I invited them to come out and watch if they wished. My plan was for a five-hour rest stop here. I was feeling well rested, but very discouraged from oversleeping.

As I was cooking, MacGill Adams mushed in with 16 young dogs. He was mushing Martin Buser's two year olds and had parked right next to my team. I noticed that he was very meticulous about his chores and was always talking to his team. MacGill had given me a box of juice at Rainy Pass and I had visited with him at Rohn where we had both taken our 24-hour rest stop. In Ophir and Iditarod, he was just arriving as I was preparing to depart.

Martin Buser, a four time Iditarod champion, has a large kennel in Big Lake, Alaska. MacGill's job was to make the Iditarod a fun experience for the younger dogs by taking longer rest stops. This adventure allowed the younger dogs to learn what the Iditarod was all about and prepared them for a potential future Iditarod.

I left Shageluk around 10 a.m. and was anxious to get to the Yukon River. Just before the Yukon, the trail went through about a half mile of willows. Suddenly about a thousand white ptarmigan took flight. With the sun shining on them and a blue sky as a backdrop, it was an amazing sight to behold. It excited the dogs and they all took off in a lope.

We soon crossed the frozen Yukon River and entered the village of Anvik. I signed in and mushed right through. The Iditarod stakes led us right back onto the Yukon River. It seemed like it was a mile wide. I was in awe of how massive it was. Occasionally we would mush by these immense riverbanks on the west side. I frequently would have visions of myself as a tiny speck moving across these vast majestic landscapes.

My dogs were used to a treeless setting and the Yukon must have seemed familiar to them. We were moving nicely as we passed a couple of teams on the way to Grayling, arriving at 8 p.m. I planned on a five-hour rest here. I bedded the dogs down and cooked for them. Hot water was available here. I had the dogs all fed, packed my sled and was ready to go in two hours.

I went inside the school building nearby and ate some soup and sandwiches that volunteers had made. I then laid down to take a two hour nap and planned to leave at 1 a.m. I blacked out again for seven hours. At this point in the race, I was trying to shorten my rest stops and pass teams that had traveled too fast in the first half of the race. I said to myself, "these oversleep rookie mistakes must end. No wonder some mushers carried alarm clocks." I bundled up for minus 45 degree Fahrenheit weather outside.

I had another 130 miles on the Yukon River and estimated I was still in around 45th position. The team was in excellent condition and moving nicely between checkpoints. They had performed beautifully on the

90-mile runs to Nikolai and Iditarod. The dogs had proven to me that they could do the longer runs without having to slow down. We departed at 6 a.m. The trail was good, and the team moved at a steady pace all day. All 11 dogs were pulling strong, arriving at the Eagle Island checkpoint at 4 p.m.

The vets were always great. They would go over each dog carefully. This vet went over my team meticulously. He noticed a couple of the dogs had swollen feet and determined that it was most likely from booties being secured too tight. He gave me some ointment to rub into their paws that would help reduce the swelling. Since the next section of trail was hard packed, I decided booties would only go on a few feet that were absolutely necessary.

After a five-hour rest, we left Eagle Island at 9 p.m. I wanted to do an all-night run to Kaltag and arrive there at daybreak. Throughout this 70-mile stretch, I struggled to stay awake. I started to hallucinate. Because of the lack of sleep, most mushers experience this at different times in the Iditarod. Even though the terrain was treeless, the horizon started looking like low branches of a tree that I found myself ducking under. I would alternate between dozing off and these hallucinations for hours throughout the night. I was lucky to have not fallen off the sled as the team just kept moving at a steady pace.

Halfway there, I became alert for a while as I passed two teams, resting alongside the trail. The team and I finally arrived in Kaltag at 6 a.m. The dogs had just covered over 130 miles with only a five-hour rest in Eagle Island. I felt very relieved that the team had performed so well. I had made up a good amount of time that I had lost from all of my oversleeping. I bedded the team down on straw and gave each dog a good hunk of lamb loaded with fat.

At the Kaltag checkpoint I found musher Rick Armstrong, who I hadn't seen since Ophir, 240 miles back. Even though we were still around 40th place, he informed me that we were still capable of finishing in the top 25. Mushers Lindwood Fiedler and Jerry Raychel were also there. I was starting to see mushers that had always been ahead of me.

I did not have a radio to listen to hourly Iditarod updates. I could only guess my position. There were usually about five to eight teams at a checkpoint, all coming and going at different times. The first few teams into a check-point received a lot of attention from spectators and the media. After the leaders left the checkpoint, the parking areas became quieter. Mushers were usually caring for their team or trying to get some much needed sleep. The short visits with other mushers were rare, but very special. Every musher respected the other, knowing that each musher was enduring the same trail and weather conditions.

There was a warm musher's cabin in Kaltag. Upstairs were bunk beds. I went right up to get some sleep. After four hours, I woke up to cook for the dogs. This was the only village I had been in when the general store was open. I bought a few candy bars and drank an orange soda pop that I was craving. I went back to the team, packed up and headed for Unalakleet at 2 p.m.

CHAPTER 8

KALTAG TO KOYUK

"You begin to understand what survival is all about when you're close to the edge, pushing yourself harder than you've ever pushed before."

Bruce Hamler – Iditasport Biker

This next 90-mile section goes from the Yukon River, over land to the village of Unalakleet, located on the west coast of Alaska. I had done this section both ways a couple years ago when I had entered the Norton Sound 200-mile sled dog race. I was glad to have finished the 150 miles on the Yukon River and was looking forward to a change in scenery.

After the initial one-hour climb out of Kaltag, the next 80-mile stretch was a gradual downhill toward the sea level town of Unalakleet. There was a light snow falling. Spruce trees were scattered about and covered with snow. The countryside was beautiful. The team was moving nicely and seemed to be enjoying the change of scenery as much as I was.

As we silently moved through this winter wonderland, I suddenly became overwhelmed with emotion. I was feeling unworthy of how blessed I was to have Penny, five thoughtful children, a career I love and the opportunity for this incredible journey. The Iditarod constantly provided me this unique solitude that was making me more aware of God's existence. I started realizing the importance of stepping back and paying more attention to the miracles of life that I so often take for granted. This solitude was a huge contrast to the busy routines at home, where I seem to have little time to step back and observe God's fingerprints that constantly surrounds us all. I am reminded of James 4:8, "Draw near to God and He will draw near to you."

After about 30 miles from reaching Unalakleet, we came to the Old Woman shelter cabin. Three dog teams were resting and parked outside. I snacked my dogs and kept going. There was more open country now and we soon found ourselves in a ground storm. The trail was completely blown in with drifting snow. Cheetah and Joe charged right through the deeper snow, meticulously following the Iditarod stakes that marked the way.

We arrived in Unalakleet at 6 a.m. Families in Unalakleet had signed up to house mushers at this checkpoint. After signing in with the checker, a snow machine led me to Junie and Linda Towarak's home. I opened up my two food bags and started boiling water to feed the team a hearty meal of ground beef. I massaged all the dogs and let them know how proud I was of them.

I had sent a lighter wooded basket sled to Unalakleet. I switched sleds and repacked. I decided to drop another dog that had a swollen foot and seemed tired. I took another gang line out and mailed it home with my second snow hook and some other gear that I would not need any more. I now had a lighter sled and an efficient string of 10 dogs.

Junie invited me into their home for breakfast. Afterward, Linda insisted that I lay down for a couple hours. I agreed only with the assurance that they would wake me in two hours. After the great rest on a bed in a warm house, I felt rejuvenated. While visiting over coffee and a sandwich, Linda handed me some smoke salmon and fried bread to take with me. It was time to go. I thanked Junie and Linda for their warm hospitality.

After eight hours in Unalakleet, Junie led me back to the trail with his snow machine at 2 p.m. The team was moving faster than they usually do leaving a checkpoint. I thought maybe they recognized the smell of the salt-water coast and it had perked them up a bit. We were getting closer to Nome and the conditions that the dogs were used to.

We struggled up some pretty steep hills out of Unalakleet. In addition to the hills, there was a cold, fierce headwind that wasn't helping. I decided to stop at the top of the very last hill. As the dogs snacked and rested behind a little knoll out of the wind, I munched on some smoked salmon and fresh fried bread that Linda had kindly given me. I took a few swigs of hot Gatorade to wash it all down.

Mushers Jerry Raychel and Dave Olesen passed by. They seemed like they were in a big hurry. The sky was clear, but this cold north wind was relentless and seemed to go right through me. I estimated the chill factor to be about -50 degrees Fahrenheit. I zipped up my survival parka to the top and pulled my fleece neck warmer so only my eyes were exposed, I then put on my down mitts over my gloves and we were off. The team descended the mountaintop through thick spruce trees. At the bottom, I saw Dave Oleson disappear into the ground storm. Jerry Raychel had to have been right in front of him. It was like mushing into a milk bottle. We were in whiteout conditions and the visibility was zero.

The snow was so deep at the bottom of the hill that we lost the trail. I estimated the head winds to be close to 40 mph and I could hardly see my leaders. I contemplated turning around and going back to camp in the spruce trees I had just come through. I would partially be out of the wind there, but it would be a long miserable night. In the hope of making it into Shaktoolik in the next two hours, I decided to press on.

The sandbar was elevated and by following it, I was quite sure that I would eventually reach Shaktoolik. I had never been on this section of trail before, but had remembered seeing this on a map. After about 40 minutes, I estimated we had gone about three miles. That meant Shaktoolik was still approximately 12 miles away.

If I looked into the howling wind, my eyes and eyelids would instantly cake up with ice. I stopped the team and went up and wiped the ice out of Cheetah and Joe's eyes. I acknowledged each dog as I hurried back to the sled. After continuing another hour, I estimated we were about seven or eight miles up the sandbar with another eight miles to go. I was scared and started to pray for protection in this life-threatening situation.

I thought of my options. It was just as close to continue to Shaktoolik seven or eight miles as it was to turn around and go back to the spruce covered hills. I thought about stopping and hunkering down in my sled. I meticulously went through the steps required. I would have to turn my sled sideways and unload everything to the leeward side of the sled. I would then climb inside my sled bag and then crawl into my sleeping bag. I didn't like that option. The dogs had been conditioned that there was always a hot meal and a bed of straw waiting for them straight ahead. I had never had to confuse my team by turning them around to go down the trail we had just traveled on.

It was getting dark now, as we continued our struggle forward. Every dog in my team had become attentive and sensed the very difficult predicament we were in. I desperately prayed for guidance. Almost immediately, Cheetah, my main leader, suddenly veered the team off the sandbar to the right, down to the lagoon ice. She then made a quick left turn. I could sense we were traveling faster. Suddenly I saw a trail stake go by. Unbelievable! Cheetah had to be feeling and sniffing her way along the trail because it was impossible to see. Dogs definitely have a sixth sense, but I was sure we were receiving some help from above, guiding my leaders to Shaktoolik. That move by Cheetah was no coincidence in these horrific blizzard conditions.

Every time we would go 200 yards without seeing a stake, I would start to panic. My focus was looking down, watching for sled marks and a trail stake. When I would finally see the sled go by one, it would assure me that Cheetah and Joe were still following the trail. Finally we went by the abandoned village of Old Shaktoolik. Junie Towarak had told me before leaving his place that this place meant Shaktoolik was two miles ahead. Junie must have known there was a blizzard in the forecast and was giving me some important information. He is a long-time resident of Alaska's west coast, an experienced dog musher and knew the dangers of coastal blizzards.

The storm continued to rage and was relentless. Cheetah and Joe were picking up speed. They must have heard the sounds of Shaktoolik and knew they were getting close. When I finally saw the first streetlight, I was only about 80 feet away from the first house. I immediately pulled the team up and set the snow hook in at the bottom of the steps.

I went up and knocked hard on the front door. It was 9 p.m. A man finally opened the door, looked at me and then noticed my team at the bottom of his steps. He exclaimed in disbelief, "you came through this storm!" I pointed Cheetah and Joe and exclaimed loud enough for him to hear me, "those two incredible leaders, miraculously brought me through it."

Shaktoolik residents like Unalakleet residents, had signed up to house particular mushers. He eventually led me about 100 yards up the beach to Walter Sookiayak's residence. We pulled in behind his house, which gave relief from the wind. After snacking and rubbing down each dog, I dug five large deep holes in the snow so each pair of dogs could curl up together out of the intense winds.

Finally I entered Walter's warm home. I was surprised to see Rick Armstrong also staying there. After hanging up my clothes to dry, Walter served me hot soup and sandwiches. I sincerely thanked him for his warm and welcoming hospitality. Walter responded by saying he felt blessed to be able to provide food and shelter, especially during this horrendous blizzard. Rick and I continued to let him know how much we appreciated his kindness. A couple years later, I was happy to repay him by putting him up at my home in Nome and buying his return airline ticket back to Shaktoolik.

Rick advised me that Joe Garnie and Lavon Barve had lost their teams in the storm, and somehow had made it into a checkpoint. Joe and Lavon were experienced and veteran Iditarod finishers. This made me feel fortunate that this hadn't happened to me. Rick continued to inform me that Terry Adkins and Gary Whittmore were somewhere out on the ice spending the night in their sleds between Shaktolik and Koyuk. Five other teams were here in Shaktoolik and several teams were hunkered down in Koyuk and Elim. Rick thought the leaders of the race were in White Mountain.

Rick was now sure if we left first out of Shaktoolik, we could place in the top 25. I immediately informed him that I felt blessed just to have survived this nightmare of a storm. I decided that it would be wise to call the National Weather Service in Nome in the morning to get a weather briefing on the forecast for our area.

As the wind continued to howl, the comfort and warmth of Walter's home gave me an overwhelming feeling of being safe and sound. There was no doubt that I had some sincere prayers of thanksgiving to give tonight. Walter enjoyed listening to Rick and I as we continued talking about the Iditarod and our experiences. I slept very comfortably on the couch in my long johns as the storm shook the house throughout the night.

The next morning Walter fixed us a hearty breakfast of pancakes, eggs, potatoes, toast and coffee. I made a call to the National Weather Service in Nome. The weatherman advised me that the trend over the next 24 hours was for improvement. I wanted assurances from him that it included local wind conditions. He again assured me that conditions throughout the Seward Peninsula would steadily improve over the next 24 hours.

That's all I wanted to hear. The conditions were still fierce outside. I told Rick that as soon as I saw the slightest improvement, I was leaving. He looked at me without saying anything. Most interior mushers are scared to death of the treeless coastal weather, for good reason. Their dogs are not use to the relentless blowing snow that causes the whiteout conditions. What Cheetah and Joe had brought me through the night before astonished me. It convinced me that God was watching over my team and I.

I went out into the storm to check on the dogs. Each pair was still curled up together. They had gotten 12 hours of sleep so I decided to cook them a hearty meal of salmon. They all ate well and went back to sleep.

The mushers that passed me yesterday on that last hill before the ground storm had eventually turned back and camped all night in the spruce trees. I somehow had passed them somewhere, but never knew it when I did. Two more Iditarod teams out of Unalakleet had stopped in the trees and joined them for the night. By mid-morning, when the four teams had better light, they decided to mush single file together through the storm. They finally arrived in Shaktoolik around 2 p.m.

I decided to start getting ready to leave. I gave the dogs some snacks and started packing up. I filled my thermos, gave all the dogs a massage, checked their feet and put booties on those who needed them. I was the first to pull out of Shaktoolik at 4 p.m. for the 60-mile mush across the ice to Koyuk. Rick pulled out right behind me. We left in 24th and 25th position. I thought Rick's prediction way back in Ophir, may surprisingly become a reality.

Joe Reddington Sr., Raymie Reddington, Dan MacEachen, Burt Bomhoff, and Linwood Fiedler were still in Shaktoolik, along with the four teams that spent the night back in the trees. We figured some would be pulling out right behind us. The visibility was now up to about two miles, but the trail was blown in and the going was slow. This open country was foreign to Rick's dogs and he asked if his team could stay close to my sled. I agreed, which meant I would be breaking trail into a head wind, for the next 60 miles into Koyuk.

Our speed gradually picked up. After about six hours, I could see the lights of Koyuk about 20 miles away. We finally arrived there at 12 a.m. Just as we were arriving in Koyuk, we watched Peryll Kyzer leaving in 20th place. Still in Koyuk were Terry Adkins, Beverly Masek and Laird Barron.

The checker also informed me that Gary Whitemore, another musher in front of me had regretfully scratched due to frostbite. He had spent the previous night out in the storm with Terry Adkins. They said there were times that Gary thought that he wouldn't make it. Many have had close calls on the Iditarod over the years and some have had to be rescued.

I bedded my team down on straw and cooked for them. They all ate well and I headed up to the community center. There was a television that everyone was gathered around. Rick Swenson was just crossing the finish line in Nome and had just become the 1991 Iditarod champion. Everyone watched with much interest. Susan Butcher had left White Mountain one hour before Rick. He eventually caught her and they tried to find the trail together in whiteout conditions. She eventually turned around and went back to White Mountain. Rick continued through the horrendous storm to win his 5th Iditarod. As of 2020, he is the only musher to have accomplished five wins.

While at the community center, I asked Karen Schmidt, who was the vet at the Koyuk checkpoint, to check out the frostbite on my wrist. It must have happened going through the storm into Shaktoolik. My clothing on my wrist had been rubbing up against it and had really bothered me on the trip into Koyuk. I was afraid it would get infected. She carefully treated and wrapped it up. The wrist was now well protected, and I sincerely thanked her.

I then ate a large bowl of hot oatmeal and drank a quart of orange juice. It is easy to get dehydrated being out in the elements 24/7. Whenever I boiled three gallons of water, I always used some of that water to mix up some powdered Gatorade in my thermos. Every couple of hours, I would drink a cup of it. This helped me to stay hydrated, to stay warm and helped me stay awake. I headed back to my dogs and started packing up for the 50 mile run to Elim. I had given the dogs a good four-hour rest and headed out at 4 a.m.

CHAPTER 9

KOYUK TO NOME

"If I died tomorrow, I'd have had a full life just running the Iditarod."

Terry Adkins – 20 Iditarod Finishes

My team started out unusually fast. We were heading directly west toward Nome and I think the dogs must have sensed we were getting closer to home. Two miles out, I passed Beverly Masek. With this pass, I had now moved into 22nd place. The 20th place finisher this particular year received $4,500 and a really nice trophy. After 20th place, a musher receives $1,000 for finishing. Suddenly 20th place seemed like a possibility.

The Iditarod is a very expensive undertaking. I had worked the previous summer driving a tour bus in Nome to help with the dog kennel expenses. I didn't have any sponsors for this race and the prize money for 20th place would cover most of my race expenses.

I arrived into Elim at 12 p.m. and Joe Garnie greeted me as I checked in. He had lost his team in the storm and searchers had not found his dogs as yet. He advised me to mush right through, but it had taken me eight hours to get there. I decided to rest for two hours before heading to White Mountain. It had to have been heartbreaking for Joe, losing his team. Joe was from Teller, a small village 70 miles from Nome. He was a friend who had made my wooded basket sled that I had switched to in Unalakleet. Joe had some impressive Iditarod finishes; 3rd in 1984, 2nd in 1986, 11th in 1987, 4th in 1988, 15th in 1989, and 9th in 1990.

After leaving Elim, I moved into 21st position. We had a long climb and steep descent off from Little Mount McKinley. I mushed right through Golovin and 18 miles later, we arrived in White Mountain at 8:35 p.m. The dogs sprinted the last 200 yards into the checkpoint. The team definitely recognized the area.

This particular year, there was a required six-hour rest in White Mountain. Every year after 1991, it became an eight-hour required rest stop. Lavon Barve had found his team and was due to leave White Mountain at 9:24 p.m. Peryll Kyzer was in 18th position and due to leave at 12:50 a.m. Terry Adkins was in 19th place and due to leave at 2:27 a.m. and Laird Barron and I were to leave eight minutes after Terry. Joe Garnie had found his team and was on his way to White Mountain. I kept telling myself, "do not make any mistakes."

I snacked the team, bedded them down and decided to let them rest for two hours before cooking for them. I was freezing. I went up to the community center to change into some dry socks and warm up. The temperature was around zero, but I was shaking and close to being hypothermic. I had run up all the hills between Elim and Golovin and my inner clothes had gotten damp. On the ice between Golovin and White Mountain, the temperature had dropped and I became chilled to the bone. I was colder coming into White Mountain than I had been anywhere else on the trail. Since leaving Anchorage, I had lost about 15 pounds of fat and that made staying warm more difficult.

I hiked up to the White Mountain Lodge. The lodge was owned by the White Mountain Native Corporation and provided a meal of the musher's choice, 'on the house.' They had a Mexican salad buffet set up. I ordered a cheeseburger and helped myself to the wide selection of salads. The salsa sauce was so good on the salad that I decided to also use it on my cheeseburger.

Terry Adkins and Laird Barron joined me at the table. Laird mentioned, "one of us would not finish in the top twenty." Terry answered, "but two of us will." I reminded them, "Joe Garnie could sneak up and surprise all three of us." We were all determined to give it our best shot. We continued sharing our stories from the trail. Reaching White Mountain was kind of a milestone, knowing we only had 77 miles to go. We were all feeling pretty proud to have made it this far.

After filling my belly, I stretched out in a lounge chair that reclined. I was so tired that it was difficult for my brain to function and organize what I had to do before leaving at my designated time. I was determined to stay awake. With three hours to go, I forced myself out of my luxurious position to get back down to my team and cook them their last hot meal. The dogs needed me as much as I needed them. It was truly a team effort. Through the many trials that a team encounters on the Iditarod, this becomes explicitly evident. The Iditarod journey enormously strengthens this bond between the musher and his dogs.

After feeding the team a hearty salmon dinner, I spent time massaging each dog and checking their feet. I placed new batteries in my headlamp. I decided to lighten my load. I placed my dog dishes, cooler, tool kit, an extra set of runners, and some extra clothing into a duffle bag to send home. My ten dogs had looked strong over the last 130 miles from Koyuk and would now have a much lighter sled to pull. They knew the trail because all of the dogs had run this 77 mile stretch many times. I was feeling excited and confident.

With twenty minutes to go. I hurried to booty my last couple of dogs as Terry Adkins took off. I finished hooking up their tug and necklines as Laird Barron was released. Finally the race judge informed me that my six hours were up. It was 2:35 a.m. I lifted the snow hook and said, "let's go." They started moving slowly and soon started building momentum. After about five miles, I passed Laird. That put me in 20th position. This was treeless country and suddenly it started snowing and the wind started howling. We found ourselves in another ground storm as I passed Terry Adkin's team. I was now in 19th place. The trail between White Mountain and Nome was frequently traveled by snow machines so was hard packed and well-marked.

We had a tail wind that would help us climb the many hills that would lead to Topkot, the largest and last hill before a steep drop, down to the coast. The blowing snow picked up and suddenly it became difficult to see the trail stakes. It was pitch dark. We were still moving at a good clip; however, the wind was now so fierce that we were again in whiteout conditions.

Three snow machines passed, heading toward White Mountain. Another snow machine stopped and the driver flagged me down. He had been drinking, was disoriented and wasn't sure which direction he was heading. I assured him he was heading to White Mountain and off he went. Suddenly another machine light appeared coming head-on at full speed. He missed my leaders and team by inches. I was exasperated. He was going so fast that if he had run over us, it would have killed several dogs.

Earlier in the race, Roger Roberts and Dave Oleson had their main leaders run over and injured around Shageluk. Later in the race out of Golovin, Rollie Westrum had his team run over by a drunk driver and one of his dogs was killed. Another year, Bob Bright was knocked out of the race by a snow machine. Tim White many years ago had to scratch when his team was run over at Cape Nome, 12 miles before reaching the finish line. Most all of these tragedies usually happen on a Friday or Saturday night when there is more alcohol consumption in the villages. I suddenly realized it was the wee hours of Saturday morning after another Friday night party. This is a continual problem on the Iditarod Trail.

Most snow machine drivers are very considerate and swing their machines in wide circles around a sled dog team. It is just a few that are irresponsible. The radio, TV, media, village leaders and all Iditarod volunteers must continue to caution and encourage villagers not to drink and drive during the race.

This close call and this sudden change in weather made me realize the race was far from over. The temperature and chill factors had dropped dramatically. I had only traveled 27 miles, but was again, chilled to the bone, even with my warmest gear on. Since Ophir, we had experienced -40 degree Fahrenheit temperatures much of the way. Some of the time, the chill factors were much lower. The tips of my toes and fingers all had a little frostbite.

By the time I reached the top of Topkot, my feet were freezing. At the bottom of Topkot, the Nome Kennel Club has a shelter cabin that is located 50 miles from Nome. The trail goes right by it. When I reached the cabin, smoke was coming out of the chimney so I decided to stop. After securing the team out of the wind and snacking each dog, I entered the one-room shelter at 6 a.m. The snow machine drivers had obviously stopped here. The cabin was empty and I was thankful for a warm fire in the wood stove.

I decided to spend one hour here to dry my socks over the stove. Bunny boots are not ventilated and my feet would get wet in them. I put a couple more logs in the wood stove, hung up my outer clothing to dry and drank some hot Gatorade.

I had not slept the past two nights since Shaktoolik (180 miles back). There was a bunk bed in the corner. I decided to lay down for an hour and then hit the trail. Even though the plywood bed was hard, it felt so good to be able to stretch out and rest. I blacked out for six hours. I was so disgusted with myself.

The cabin was shaking as the wind howled noisily outside. It was now a full-fledged blizzard. I put some more wood into the wood stove. I then went outside to snack the dogs. They were all snuggled up to one another. I brought in more firewood from outside. I estimated the winds out of the East were close to 50 mph. Having lived on the west coast of Alaska for the past 25 years, I knew this weather was not a local condition, but instead, a storm that was widespread over most of the western coast of Alaska. These storms come in a series, with usually a nice day in between. This one was the third storm in less than a week that followed this pattern. I decided to stay put and hoped it would let up.

Mushing through this area many times, I realized if this wind had been a North wind, it would most likely be a local condition, known as the Solomon blowhole. Hellacious winds would funnel down the Solomon River valley and then would flare out for about 25 miles on this coastal stretch. A musher can mush through the blow-hole winds knowing it will gradually improve when you reach the Safety checkpoint. I found myself wondering if that was how Safety Roadhouse got its name.

Terry Adkins and Laird Barron would have been about 30 minutes behind me when I had reached the cabin. I figured they saw my team and quietly passed by. It was about a 25-mile mush to Safety. I figured they would have reached Safety about 9 a.m. Joe Garnie could have gone by as well. I figured I was now in 21st or 22nd place.

I became very restless. I swept the floor and cleaned the cabin. I went outside to check on the dogs and was about blown away. Back in the cabin, I forced myself to lay down for a couple more hours. I woke up and put more wood in the wood stove. I ate smoked salmon, made some warm oatmeal and drank lots of Gatorade. At 4 p.m., something inside me was telling me to go. I would look outside and the storm was telling me to stay. I would snack the dogs every four or five hours. I laid back down and fell asleep again.

At 9 p.m., I woke up again and it was pitch black out. The storm had let up a bit so I decided to go. The wind was still strong and fortunately it would be a tail wind, meaning the mush to Safety would be much easier for the dogs, especially after a 15-hour rest. I checked my headlamps and they both had plenty of battery life. I bundled up and went outside to pack the sled. I gave the dogs their last bag of snacks and hooked up the team. I was out of snacks for the dogs, but knew there was a large burlap bag of dog food waiting in Safety. I pulled the snow hook and we were off.

The team was moving fast along the hard packed trail. There was an occasional drift, but they were minor. The visibility was still zero, but the Iditarod trailbreakers had positioned the trail stakes much closer together through this stretch of trail. As my rested team went zipping toward Safety, I realized I should have left much sooner. My only hope was that Terry and Laird were still waiting out the storm in Safety.

I arrived there at midnight. The checker informed me that Terry and Peryl Kyzer had been in Safety all day and had pulled out just two hours before my arrival in 18th and 19th position. He also let me know that Laird Barron had never arrived. I figured the poor guy must have weathered the storm for 15 hours in his sled somewhere between White Mountain and the Topkot cabin.

That put me back in 20th position. I decided to snack my dogs some frozen salmon and ground beef and give them a bit of a rest. I was still having a hard time staying warm so I went inside to have some hot chocolate. After 30 minutes, it was time to get to Nome and claim the 20th place that was waiting for me. The team took right off at my command. It was still storming, but the tailwind made the last 22 miles much easier for my 10 strong finishers.

I started feeling goose bumps with about eight miles to go, when the lights of Nome became visible. I was overjoyed that we were this close. By the team's rapid pace, I knew they were as excited as I. I had spent almost every hour, day and night, the past two weeks with these special animals. Considering all we had been through; it had been an incredible experience. It would soon be over, however, there was this lingering desire, wishing it wouldn't end.

This adventure had been challenging and exhausting, but at the same time, the experience had been an awakening of sorts. I had learned a lot more about myself. From all that I witnessed and felt, I was much more aware and assured of God's existence. Priorities had been sorted out. I had become much more thankful for all that I am blessed with.

Two miles out of town, a couple cars had come out to welcome us in. Eventually the trail led us off the ice and onto Front Street. People were gathering as the team trotted the last 300 yards. Finally, Cheetah and Joe led me right into the chute area and we knew it was suddenly over. It was 3 a.m. and considering the time, I was surprised there were so many people that were out to welcome me home. It was so good to see Penny. She had helped make this incredible experience possible. We joyfully embraced. It was emotional. Penny snacked and stroked each dog. The race official made sure I had all the required gear in my sled. Over the loud speaker, the Nome mayor, Leo Rasmussen, who was also the Nome checker, announced my 20th place and finishing time of 14 days, 19 hours and 38 minutes. It had been the toughest two weeks I had ever experienced, but one that had dramatically impacted my life.

CHAPTER 10

REFLECTIONS

"I'll say one thing: you finish this race and you feel like you could spit in a tiger's eye."

Terry Adkins – 20 Iditarod Finishes

Of the 75 mushers that started the 1991 Iditarod, 60 finished. This particular Iditarod was especially challenging. A thrilling ride down the steps into Happy River Canyon, a ground storm over Rainy Pass, a hairy scary ride down the Dalzell Gorge, a near sled breaking adventure getting out of the Alaska Range, minus 40 and 50 degree temperatures for half the race, and if that wasn't enough, three coastal blizzards over the last 250 miles. Unfortunately, these conditions had a factor in 15 teams not finishing. The 60 teams that did finish, it took them between 12 and 22 days to reach Nome. Ten of those teams took 21 to 22 days to cross the finish line.

Success on the Iditarod means a combination of many factors. Sleep deprivation and the incredible demands that constantly arise can tremendously affect a musher's response. Mushers that are well prepared, flexible and stay positive, have a much better chance of accomplishing their particular goals.

Puppy training is important as well. Two different years, our female dog Daisy was in 'heat' when the Iditarod Champion Joe Runyan finished. That was an advantage of living in Nome. Those two years, Joe agreed to breed his leader, Ferlin to Daisy (For a fee). Daisy's litters were born in May. Our children gave the puppies a lot of attention during the summer months. This results in dogs that are very friendly and comfortable around people. By breeding strong Iditarod finishers, the puppies usually end up very strong and desirable sled dogs with incredible heart.

In addition, many days during the summer, our son Thurman would open the large puppy pen gate and the puppies would chase after him for a mile or two. This enormously strengthened their muscles and lung capacities during this very fast growing period. Cleanliness is important as well. While he was running them, someone would clean out the puppy pen. The high protein puppy food and water pans were always full throughout the day to meet their fast growing diet needs.

Using mature and experienced sled dogs is a huge factor in the success of a team. Mushers also look for dogs with good tough feet, good eaters, fast trotters, dogs that rebound quickly and are powerful pullers with lots of heart. Having good leaders that listen, love to be in front and can't wait to see what's over the next hill, may be the most important ingredient. Lavon Barve once said, "about 25 out of 100 sled dogs will lead. Eight to twelve of those 25 will be good leaders and three out of those 25 will be excellent leaders." I would definitely classify Cheetah and Joe as excellent leaders.

A training program that gets the dogs in excellent physical and mental condition is another plus. This can be a complicated puzzle in itself. What works for some, does not work for others. Keeping the dogs happy by training on a variety of trails, snacking at the right time and giving them lots of attention are all essential in how strong a bond that is developed between the musher and dogs.

The proper diet is also important and can be confusing to put together. Water is very critical in preventing dehydration. If a dog's urine is too yellow, that can quickly tell you if a particular dog needs more water. Sometimes I had to trick a dog into drinking by adding some warm fish soup, which my dogs always loved. The dogs burn a lot of calories every day, so fat is very important ingredient in their diet. Lamb contains a lot of fat and I snacked it often. Chicken skins also had a good amount of fat that I added to some of their hot meals. My dogs seemed to like ground beef as well. In addition, the team loved salmon and white fish, frozen or cooked. No matter what, it is important on the Iditarod to have a wide variety of food at each checkpoint.

First aid and caring for each dog is another huge factor in a musher's success. Examining each dog's feet at every checkpoint is crucial. Vets are always available.

Treating a dog immediately for diarrhea, vomiting, and injuries, will many times allow the dog to recover quickly and stay in the race. Sometimes I would give dogs a ride in the sled and afterward, they were raring to go.

Today (2020), there isn't an animal on earth that has the stamina and endurance that an Iditarod sled dog has. Since the first Iditarod in 1973, mushers have been breeding the leaders and dogs that finish strong for them. Over the last 45+ years of the race, an Iditarod sled dog has emerged that runs faster, longer and recovers quicker with less rest. Just like the mushers, the dogs love seeing a new and different trail every day.

The Iditarod is an incredible test of toughness and stamina for the dogs and mushers. Driving a dog team across the vast Alaskan wilderness was exhilarating and at the same time, demanding and exhausting. The experience was filled with beauty, challenges and strategies. There were powerful emotions that would frequently penetrate my total being. For me, it had truly been a majestic journey, physically, mentally, emotionally and spiritually.

In the 1996 Iditarod Annual, the late Bill Vauldrin, who ran the 1974 and 1975 Iditarods, describes the Iditarod better than anyone ever has. He wrote, "THIS IS THE IDITAROD: UNSPEAKALBLE BEAUTY, MIXED WITH VERY REAL PAIN. It's also life, in a nutshell. It's how it is, and always will be—probably, even how it should be. Pleasure unearned is pleasure unappreciated. It's the things we work for, suffer for, that give us lasting satisfaction."

Vauldrin continued, "the Iditarod appeals to everything in me...passing your eyes over all the incredible country stretched out to the horizon in every direction…. the hills and trees and rivers and valleys….all the country will be yours. It will belong to you in a way that no one could ever diminish, because you will have penetrated to the heart of it—and become a part of it—and it will have become a part of you. Forever."

Vauldrin concludes, "I know that someday, I'm going to look back over all the things I've done in my life. Among the few I know I'll never be sorry for, was running the Iditarod."

I felt the same way and realized it would have never happened if Penny had not insisted, "1991 should be the year".

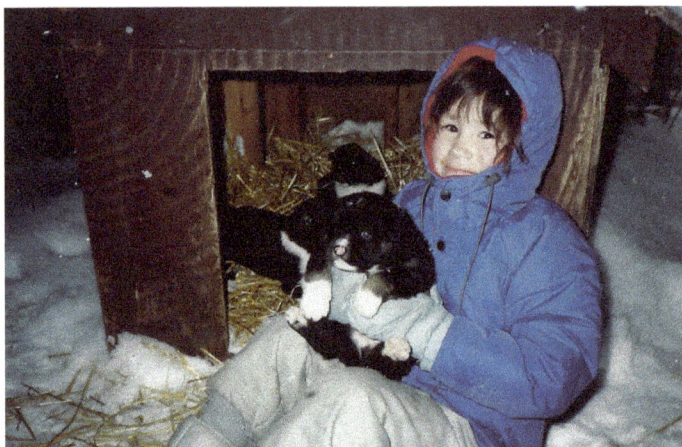

My daughter Dana, showing a litter some love. Some of the dogs
we were using on the Iitarod, came from this liter.

The dogs were excited. Whenever we loaded them in the truck,
they knew they would soon be going for a run.
This time, however, they were headed to the airport for
an hour flight to Anchorage.

Penny and I were excited and anxious for the race to start in Anchorage. The dogs were taking great interest in their new surroundings. They were loving all the attention they were getting. Just like us, they love seeing and experiencing new things. At the same time, they knew they would soon be doing what they love to do.

We stopped at Mark's place for a two hour rest,
on our way to Wasilla for the restart.

My son Thurman is comforting Cheetah and
Joe at the starting line in Anchorage.

After a four-hour rest, Cheetah on the right and Joe on the left,
lead us as we charged out of Wasilla. I control them by my voice.
For turns, we use the old horse commands; 'Gee' means turn
right, 'Haw' means turn left, 'On By' means keep going.

It was a beautiful sight arriving onto the Happy River. I was a little shook up after watching my sled do a 360 degree turn in mid air as it flew off the top of step 3. The river offered a great place to snack the dogs and take a quick break. In comparison to my condition, the dogs were all fine and seemed to have enjoyed the step challenge. Photo © by Jeff Schultz/SchultzPhoto.com

It was a long climb and a milestone, reaching the summit of
Rainy Pass in a snow storm. The dogs picked up speed as we
rounded the top. One advantage of mushing through falling snow
is the dogs stay well hydrated. Notice the stake in the picture that
help guide the team leaders and I along the Iditarod Trail.
Photo © by Jeff Schultz/SchultzPhoto.com

It was a beautiful, but hairy scary ride through the Dalzell Gorge.
Photo © by Jeff Schultz/SchultzPhoto.com

Jerry Holtshouser watching me pack my sled as the dogs finish their 12 hour rest stop in McGrath.

My toboggan sled all packed ready to leave McGrath

A special moment with Cheetah and Joe before leaving Iditarod. There is a special bond that I had with Cheetah and Joe. When they were three months old, I would let them run free, chasing after me on my ATV four-wheeler. The two of them always wanted to be in front of all their littermates. This alerted me that they may be natural leaders. When they were a year old, I started running them in lead with an older experienced leader. They learned my voice commands quicker that way. They started winning races when they were one and a half years old. Cheetah and Joe were strong, smart and had developed into incredible leaders.

After I overslept in Grayling, I and the dogs were well rested for a long 130 mile run up the never-ending Yukon River. The river starts in Canada and is 2,000 miles long. As the dogs moved me along on the snow covered ice, I thought about how dangerous this raging river would be in a couple months. I then started thinking about what the boats looked like on the Yukon, hundreds of years ago. My dogs were swiftly moving up the river. I think the treeless Yukon reminded them of the treeless country around Nome that my dogs were use to. Photo © by Jeff Schultz/SchultzPhoto.com

I often felt like a speck, mushing through these vast landscapes. At the same time, it was exhilarating, moving across this countryside without a motor driven vehicle. This is the way people traveled for thousands of years. It gave me a sense of being self reliant. I better understand why the Amish still use horses for transportation and grow their own food. Living in Alaska the past 53 years, I have observed a large part of the population hunting, fishing and living a subsistent lifestyle. This is a very satisfying and rewarding way to live.
Photo © by Jeff Schultz/SchultzPhoto.com

I loved mushing through the winter wonderland on the 90 mile portage between Kaltag and Unalakleet. We were now heading west. Dogs possess an amazing sense of direction. I noticed my team had picked up their pace. They sensed we were heading home. I was also in a happy mood on this trail to Unalakleet. Their rapid pace was another indication that they were sensing my mood and enjoying the scenery as much as I was. Photo © by Jeff Schultz/SchultzPhoto.com

Mushers become very alert watching and encouraging their leaders during a ground storm. One time on a training run, I found myself lost in white out conditions. I was not on any trail. I was about eight miles from home, running my team across some open country, and a storm had moved into the area very quickly. I simply commanded my leaders, "lets go home." My leaders turned and an hour later, they had us back to our dog lot. These sled dogs are incredible animals.

Photo © by Jeff Schultz/SchultzPhoto.com

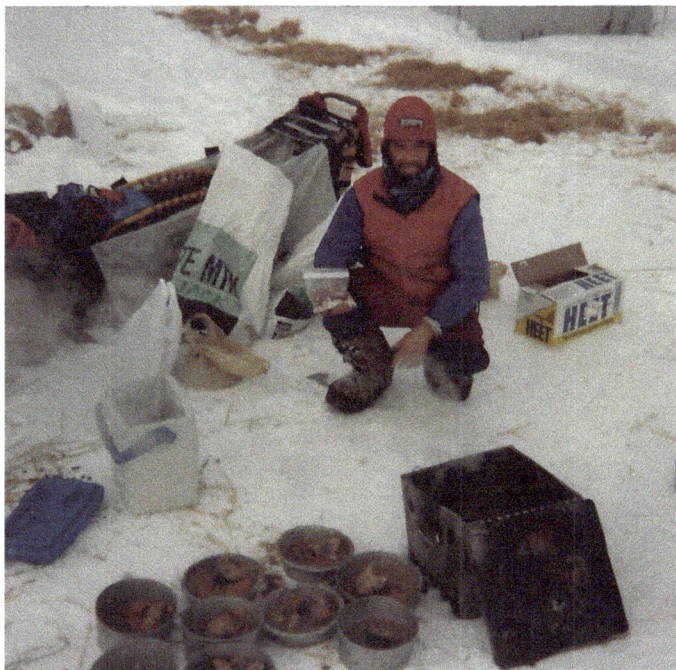

The dogs looked strong coming into White Mountain. The team had passed over 24 dog teams over the past 200 miles. We were now in 21st place., which was surprising since I had overslept so many times. I decided to reward the ten remaining dogs with a gourmet salmon dinner. We were now only 77 miles from the finish line. I was upset about how much I had overslept, but very proud of how well my dogs had performed.

The previous page has a picture of a dog team entering the Iditarod finish line in Nome. When the nose of the lead dog finally crosses under the 'Burl Arch', it signifies the triumphant end of another team's long and epic journey.

Photo (C) by Jeff Schultz/SchultzPhoto.com

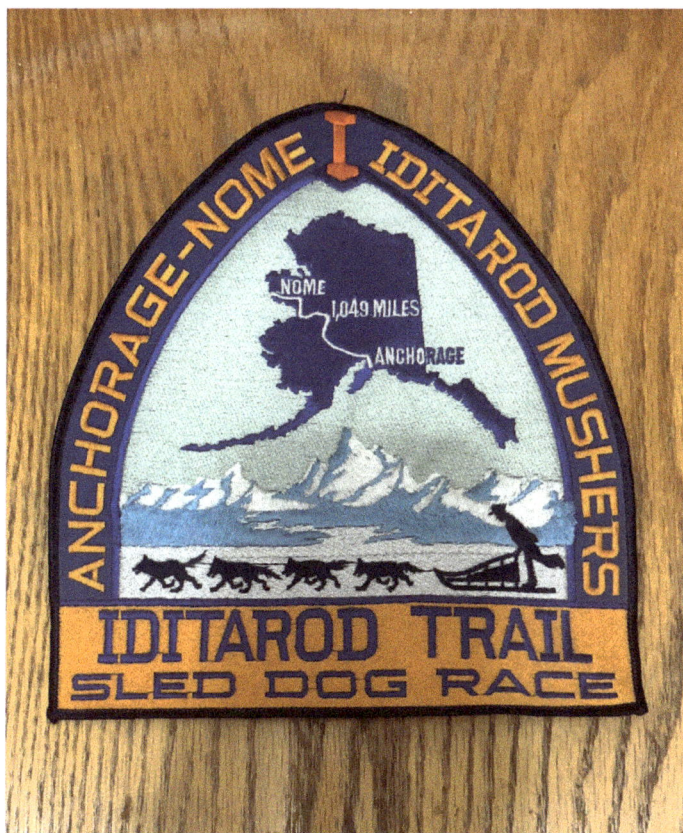

My treasured and coveted Finisher Patch that all Iditarod finishers receive. It is large enough to place on the back of a coat.

My champions, Cheetah on my right and Joe on my left.

AFTERWORD

I soon decided after doing the southern route of the Iditarod in 1991, to do the northern route in 1992. It would be about 300 different miles that I was anxious to see and experience. I also wanted to try and travel over the terrain in daylight that I had done at nighttime the year before.

The late Herbie Nayokpuk, a 10-time Iditarod finisher known as the Shishmaref Cannonball, once told me, "there's something about the Iditarod that makes a musher want to do it again." I was definitely experiencing that desire to do better, but something a lot more powerful was drawing me back to the race. Riding the sled runners behind these incredible sled dogs was part of it. I also loved challenges and the Iditarod offered plenty of those. In addition, I was being drawn back to all the alone time that I experienced on the trail. It had been a spiritual awakening of sorts and I treasured this solitude that the Iditarod so abundantly provided.

Penny and I went through another hectic three months preparing for the race. I had purchased a couple more dogs from Susan Butcher to strengthen my team. I felt more confident from what I had learned in the 1991 race. Another successful Iditarod finisher told me, "after your dogs get an eight hour rest on the Iditarod, you basically have a brand new team." I realized I had taken way too many 12-hour rest stops. I decided to reduce those 12-hour stops to five and eight hour rest stops. I was confident that this was the necessary strategy for a top 10 finish.

Once the race started, the team performed beautifully, arriving in Nicolai in eighth place. Unfortunately, a few of my dogs came down with the stomach flu, creating the 'runs' and the refusal to eat. It slowly went through the team for the next 250 miles. The vets administered medicine to help slow down the 'runs,' but it didn't help much.

I started carrying a couple dogs at a time and had to take too many 12-hour rests at each checkpoint. Due to this stomach flu, I had to drop a few of the dogs along the way, including my powerful leader, Joe. It was a devastating reminder that things do not always go as planned on the Iditarod.

When we had reached Ruby, the nine dogs that remained, were finally over the flu and started eating like starved wolves. At this point, I wish I had not dropped my lead dog Joe, back in McGrath. Even without Joe, the team started moving much quicker. We passed about 25 teams over the last 400 miles and ended up in a respectable, 27th place. Cheetah again proved to me how reliable she was as a leader, running those last 400 miles in single lead.

I continued to run my team in local races over the next two years. In 1994, I decided that raising a family, teaching school full time, coaching the high school basketball team and taking care of a dog team 365 days out of the year, was too much. It was a hard decision, but I finally decided to sell the dog team. One Iditarod musher bought seven of my dogs including Joe. Local mushers bought the others. I kept Cheetah and she lived to be 14.

I now enjoy watching the Iditarod ceremonial start every year at different locations in Anchorage. It brings back many memories, but also stirs something deep inside me. I find myself a bit envious, wishing to experience the Iditarod one more time. Instead, I go home, type in Iditarod.com on my computer and join the 'Insider.' I then enjoy reliving the race by following all the mushers to Nome via satellite.

Penny and I now have a total of 11 grandchildren. That means I will most likely have many great grandchildren after I have left this world. I would love to have known about my granddads and great granddads that were gone before I was born. One of the motivations to write this book was to give my great grandchildren a chance to learn a bit about their great granddad and possibly inspire them to new adventures.

I have lived a very active life, playing sports and running all through high school and college. Most of my adult life, I ran 10Ks, marathons and triathlons. During my late 60s, my knees could not take running anymore so I started hiking. Five years ago, when I turned 70 years old, I decided to hike the Appalachian Trail. My goal was to hike at least 2000 miles of it. Maybe my desire for solitude had something to do with it. You can read about this adventure in my book: "Perseverance" by Bill Jack. It is available in paperback from: amzn.com/1594338787 or on Kindle: amzn.com/dp/B07TD6TFX3

You may purchase a signed copy by emailing me at: billjack24@hotmail.com

Since my Appalachian Trail adventure, I still love being outside, immersing myself in the wonders of nature and the miracles of life. Often times it is a four or five mile walk, doing yard work, splitting wood for winter or snow blowing our long driveway. Being physically active is a huge part of my DNA and I find it to be highly therapeutic. I treasure my solitude and the peace and enjoyment it brings me. At the same time, I love my social life, especially a round of golf on a golf course somewhere.

My Instagram: Holcomb.on.the.at

1991 RACE RESULTS

Musher	Days-Hrs-Min	Purse
1. Rick Swenson	12:16:34	$50,000
2. Martin Buser	12:18:41	$39,500
3. Susan Butcher	12:21:59	$32,000
4. Tim Osmar	12:22:33	$25,500
5. Joe Runyan	12:22:36	$19,000
6. Frank Teasley	13:12:27	$15,000
7. DeeDee Jonrow	13:13:44	$14,000
8. Matt Desalernos	13:13:44	$13,000
9. Rick Mackey	13:13:54	$12,000
10. Bill Cotter	13:13:57	$11,000
11. Kate Persons	13:14:20	$9,500
12. Jeff King	13:14:24	$9,000
13. Jacques Philip	13:15:07	$8,500
14. Jerry Austin	13:17:10	$8,000
15. Michael Madden	13:20:06	$7,500

Musher	Days-Hrs-Min	Purse
16. Ketil Reitan	13:21:54	$6,500
17, Lavon Barve	13:22:20	$6,000
18. Peryll Kyzer	14:16:26	$5,500
19. Terry Adkins	14:16:46	$5,000
20. Bill Jack	14:19:38	$4,500
21. Beverly Masek	15:09:03	
22. Laird Barron	15:10:07	All mushers
23. Joe Garnie	15:11:53	that finished
24. Rick Armstrong	15:12:24	after 20th
25. Lindwood Fiedler	15:23:45	received
		$1,000
26. Burt Bomhoff	16:08:48	
27. Dan MacEachen	16:09:08	
28. Dave Olesen	16:10:01	
29. Raymie Redington	16:10:02	
30. Dave Allen	16:10:25	
31. Joe Redington Sr.	16:11:56	
32. Jerry Raychel	16:17:51	
33. Mark Nordman	16:17:55	
34. Malcolm Vance	17:09:30	
35. Macgill Adams	17:10:10	
36. Nikolai Ettyne	17:10:53	
37. Alexander Reznyik	17:11:54	
38. Tony Shoogukwruk	17:12:34	
39. Rollin Westrum	17:13:44	

Musher	Days-Hrs-Min	Purse
40. Brian Stafford	17:15:35	
41. John Suter	17:18:23	
42. Roger Roberts	17:22:08	
43. Larry Munoz	17:22:59	
44. Jim Cantor	18:00:02	
45. Terry Seaman	18:00:08	
46. Kazuo Kojima	18:00:29	
47. Rich Bosela	18:00:50	
48. Pat Danly	18:02:23	
49. Dave Breuer	18:04:49	
50. Chris Converse	18:05:09	
51. Sepp Herrman	21:05:59	
52. Lynda Plettner	21:21:04	
53. Jon Terhune	22:00:11	
54. Gunner Johnson	22:00:57	
55. Urtha Lenharr	22:01:05	
56. Tom Daily	22:01:06	
57. Mark Williams	22:01:06	
58. Catherine Mormile	22:01:18	
59. Don Mormile	22:01:35	
60. Brian O'Donoghue	22:05:55	

31 Iditarod Trivia Questions

How many can you answer after reading *Majestic Journey?*

www.iditarod.com

This informative site is filled with pictures and educational materials and lesson plans for teachers to use the first two weeks of March. A great way for educators to provide a fun and exciting two week unit for their students.

1 . Who was the first musher to win five Iditarods?
2 . How old does a musher have to be to enter the Iditarod?
3 . Who and how old was the oldest musher to finish the Iditarod?
4 . Where in Alaska does Iditarod musher Martin Buser live?
5 . Who and in what year did the first female musher win the Iditarod race?
6 . In 1991, where was the official starting line?
7 . In 2020, where was the official starting line?
8 . How many days did it take Dick Wilmarth to win the first Iditarod in 1973?
9 . Who took 32 days to finish the 1973 Iditarod? The Red Lantern each year is awarded to the last finisher, which symbolizes that musher's perseverance.
10 . Who and what years were the first father/son champions?

11 . What state is Terry Adkins from?

12 . Who was the first Iditarod Champion from Norway?

13 . Name the female musher who won four Iditarod championships.

14 . Who was the first musher to win the 1000 mile Yukon Quest and the Iditarod in the same year?

15 . What two countries does the Yukon Quest travel through?

16 . What town in Alaska is the Iditarod Headquarters located?

17 . Who are known as the father and mother of the Iditarod?

18 . What 400 mile sled dog race was run in Nome from 1908 to 1917?

19 . Iditarod teams travel on what river for approximately 150 miles?

20 . What checkpoint do most mushers end their Iditarod?

21 . What village is the first Iditarod checkpoint on Alaska's west coast?

22 . What river do mushers travel on between the Nicolai and McGrath?

23 . Where do mushers reach the highest elevation on the Iditarod?

24 . What village do mushers enter when they leave the Yukon River?

25 . Where is the last checkpoint before Nome?

26 . Over the last 250 miles of the Iditarod, what checkpoint are mushers required to take an eight hour rest?

27 . When mushers take the northern route on even years, where is the first checkpoint on the Yukon River?

28 . When mushers take the southern route on odd years, what checkpoint comes after Ophir?

29 . For the lead dogs to turn right, a musher yells _____.

30 . What is the first checkpoint after leaving the Dalzell Gorge?

31. Who finished 20th in the 1991 Iditarod?

(Answers on page 127)

Websites Promoting Dog Mushing

www.iditarod.com
Iditarod Headquarters - Wasilla, Alaska

www.turningheadskennel.com
Travis Beals and Sarah Stokey - Seward, Alaska

www.spkennel.com
Aliy Zirkle and Allen Moore - Two Rivers, Alaska

www.sivoracingkennel.com
Joar Ulsom - Willow, Alaska

www.teampetit.com
Nicolas Petit - Girdwood, Alaska

www.buserdog.com
Martin Buser - Big Lake, Alaska

www.trailbreakerkennel.com
David Monson - Fairbanks, Alaska

www.17th-dog.com
Matthew and Liz Failor - Willow, Alaska

www.deedeejonrowe.com
Dee Dee Jonrowe - Willow, Alaska

www.schultzphoto.com
Jeff Schultz - Anchorage, Alaska

Answers To The Trivia Questions

1 . Rick Swenson

2 . Eighteen

3 . Norman Vaughan, 84

4 . Big Lake

5 . Libby Riddles, 1985

6 . Anchorage

7 . Willow

8 . Twenty

9 . John Schultz

10 . Dick Mackey 1978, Rick Mackey 1983

11 . Montana

12 . Robert Sorlie

13 . Susan Butcher

14 . Lance Mackey

15 . United States and Canada

16 . Wasilla

17 . Joe Redington and Dorothy Page

18 . The All Alaskan Sweep-stakes

19 . Yukon River

20 . Nome

21 . Unalakleet

22 . Kuskokwim River

23 . Rainy Pass

24 . Kaltag

25 . Safety

26 . White Mountain

27 . Ruby

28 . Iditarod

29 . Gee

30 . Rohn

31 . Bill Jack

Bill Jack
billjack24@hotmail.com

Available for book signings, readings, other book events,
and to speak to schools, clubs, and organizations.